FROM
BROKE
^{TO} BOLD

A Testimony Into Real Estate Through
Faith, Family, and Business

ASHER CARR

DEDICATION

To the love of my life, the anchor
that keeps me steady.
To my Loving Mother and Healthy Father
that nurtured and loved me.
To my Wealthy Father that instilled
the wisdom I have today.
And most of all,
To my Lord and Savior Jesus Christ
who directed my steps
in becoming **BOLD**

CONTENTS

COMMISSIONED: A DAY TO REMEMBER

SURVIVING
BROKE

CHAPTER 1

The End is Where We Begin- June 14, 2019

My heart was racing, sweat was soaking up my shirt, fatigue was setting in, and I was only 10 minutes into it. I couldn't believe that jumping around on a trampoline made me feel like death after a few minutes. It was the most intense workout I'd done since Army ROTC (Reserve Officer in Training Corp), and the hardest obstacle I faced in the program was running a 10K route five times for our morning workouts in Ranger Club. I wanted to leave, and yet I was right where I needed to be for the time being. Instead of taking a "normal" lunch break, I decided to tap into my inner gymnast and work out at a local trampoline park close to my office. This was my third day jumping at this park and I was feeling motivated. Every jump brought me back to my days as a Penn State cheerleader- good times! The workouts were so good that I decided to get a summer pass from June to August for only $30. Unlimited jumps throughout the summer. Unfortunately, I was limited to an hour that day and I had to head back to the office soon.

Since November of 2017, I was working as a financial analyst at a private wealth company. My main responsibilities included data quality and running various reports for the tax cost department. Our team spearheaded the formation of 1099 tax forms for the ultra-wealthy. Every day was just another day of digging into a portfolio and changing the numbers on their assets, so they could be reported correctly for tax season. In short, I was a glorified Certified Public Accountant in a private company. It wasn't the sexiest job and yet it paid well for my age.

When I got back to my desk from the trampoline park, I continued working on a special project assigned to me. It was taking longer than planned to complete yet I found a flow in finishing it and I was nearly done. I was happy about the progress and I couldn't wait to present the final presentation to my leadership.

Suddenly, my manager, Joe, stopped by my cubicle and asked, "Asher, can Tom and I meet with you for a second?"

"Sure", I said.

Joe was the President of the Tax Cost Department. He was the last person I interviewed with in my three round interview process and we connected well through our common interest in enhancing procedures and systems for analysts. In my first few months, he assigned me various business-as-usual tasks and during tax season, and I worked with him and the rest of the six-person department on data quality control on weekends. After tax season, it's back to the normal business-as-usual flow. After a year in, I reported to my supervisor, Tom, and I didn't work with Joe as much. Tom was my direct supervisor, and he was great. He was hired a few months after I was brought in and he had great energy and always made sure I had everything I needed.

I was surprised to hear from Joe. I haven't spoken to Joe since tax season ended in April and suddenly, he wanted to talk? And why was Tom involved? I thought we were all going to meet in Tom's office down the hall from my desk and we ended up walking down to a conference room in Human Resources (HR) on the first floor. When the conference door opened, I saw the faces of the two HR ladies I had connected well with since I got hired. I knew right away something was wrong.

Joe got right to it, "Asher, we've determined that this relationship isn't cohesive and as a result, we are letting you go as of today. We appreciate everything you've done for us and we wish you the best in whatever you do next."

I replied, "Ok. Thank you."

The men walked back upstairs to tell the rest of the team I was being let go.

I couldn't believe it. I didn't know what was going on. I was doing what I was supposed to do and yet I was being let go a week after my 25th birthday. Trish, the Director of HR, told me the next steps of the process, including the paperwork, and what to expect. Then Rachel, who was Trish's right hand woman, escorted me back to my desk to grab my belongings, clear my desk, and then escorted me out to the parking lot. As I gave her my key fob, there was only a sense of confusion, sadness, and embarrassment running through my body.

I walked to my car, packed my stuff in the backseat, and started the car. As soon as I drove off the lot and onto the Garden State Parkway, I had a surge of emotion I hadn't felt in a while.... **LIBERATION!**

I screamed joy and happiness throughout my drive back home and I blasted music so loud, I should've gotten a ticket.

I WAS FREE! God heard my prayers and He answered them. Although it wasn't in the way I'd expected, God knows all things and I knew that I had the opportunity to get on the path I was working toward the last year; becoming a real estate professional. What a day!

As I was winding down and taking in the events that had transpired, I noticed something very interesting in all this; June 14th, 2019 was the day I was let go from my job and June 15th, 2020 was the day I planned on having my wedding ceremony in the Dominican Republic. Was this a coincidence?

Of course, I told my fiancé, Janay, what had happened and to my surprise, she took it better than I expected. I felt that it was my sense of faith and hope that assured her that this was temporary, and we would still have our wedding as planned. This wasn't the ideal situation we expected and yet this was the beginning of the end of a "normal" life.

My name is Asher and I am broke.

CHAPTER 2

This is a Warning, A Courtesy Call- July 8, 2019

Despite being well-paid for entering digits for the ultra-wealthy, I should've anticipated my exit out of finance to be sooner rather than later. After my first tax season, I knew I didn't want to be there forever. Did I learn a lot about tax breaks of all types? Sure. Did I build a skillset in streamlining processes for quality assurance? You betcha. Did I nearly work myself so much that I ripped three of my best dress pants because I loaded up on carbs eating Italian food on the weekends at the office? Yep. Don't get me wrong, working in financial operations had its perks and it wasn't all bad. It was my attitude that led me to my downfall in the industry and I was eager to focus on real estate.

A month later, I was hanging out at home playing Call of Duty: Modern Warfare 3 and just relaxing. After an hour of gaming, I looked at my Linkedin messages and saw a notification from the Vice President of a real estate company in Hoboken. Ever since I got let go, I was relentlessly applying for real estate operation positions in the New York City Metro Area. Little did I know that this Linkedin connection would change the course of my destiny.

I can't remember his name and yet the phone call was just what I needed to get me going in the right direction. On the call, I remember talking about my goals in real estate, which was to build an investment portfolio on the side while helping a real estate team build and operate efficiently and effectively. He admired my ambition and gave me his insight: "If you want to contribute at a high level, you should get your real estate license". Now, I've tackled the idea of getting licensed since last year. When I got into real estate investing, a real estate license was optional.

My interest in real estate started when my step dad, aka Wealthy Dad, shared the idea of real estate investing with me in late 2017. I call him my Wealthy Dad because he taught me everything I needed to know about personal development since I was a kid. When I was in third grade, he started to teach me money concepts from the book, *Rich Dad, Poor Dad* by Robert Kiyosaki. He even got the Cashflow for Kids boardgame for my brother and I, and it complimented the book's message about assets and liabilities. At that time, I had no idea what the material meant, and it was clear I didn't pick up the money habits he tried to instill in me. However, all of that content came into full circle during my college career when I switched my major from hospitality management to entrepreneurship. Instead of working in a hotel, why don't I just own one, I thought. My Wealthy Dad was always passionate about teaching my brother and me strong success habits and mindsets to become wealthy in every aspect of life. While I was in finance, he felt that I would be successful in real estate investing part-time through buying and holding real estate. This form of real estate investing is purchasing a home, holding it as a rental property, and generating monthly cash flow from the rental. AirBnb is a popular platform to create such an income. My Wealthy Dad also showed me homes in one of the most expensive zip codes in New Jersey; Alpine. These homes were typically massive mansions at high-end luxury prices, minutes away from New York City. One listing we looked at on Zillow was priced at $32,000,000, and it was incredible. I was inspired to get a home there one day, and at the time, I didn't need a real estate license to do it. Or so I thought.

The Vice President told me that even as an administrative associate, it would be better for me to have a license to know how an agent operates, what laws they needed to know, and more importantly, have more access to resources and opportunities I wouldn't get as an unlicensed associate.

After our phone call, I googled the nearest real estate schools in the area and I signed up for a course at the Real Estate School of Montclair. Class started the next day, and I was eager, ready and willing to do what it took to be a licensed agent.

CHAPTER **3**

Get to the Grind- July 9, 2019

I woke up the next morning with much anticipation for the start of getting my real estate license. I didn't know what to expect and yet I knew that I was headed in the right direction for a new career.

When I got to class, it was like any other first day of school feeling. You don't know anyone; everyone is awkwardly silent looking confused, and you don't know where to sit. For me, this wasn't a problem. I always make it a point to sit as close as possible to the front to get the most out of the classroom experience. So, sure enough, I grabbed the endrow-desk of the first row, and waited for the instructor to start the class. I was ready to learn about real estate. The instructor, Mercure, was very sweet and eager to get us through the content over the next month. For a New Jersey real estate license, students need to complete 75 hours of real estate education, pass the school exam, and then pass the national exam. I knew completing the full 75 hours would be a challenge because I had plans to attend a church convention that happened during the last week of classes. Fortunately, the instructor said that students needed at least 60 hours to take the school test and I would meet that requirement by the time I flew out to the convention.

The first day of class was mostly an orientation day and a glance over the first two chapters. For the month, however, we would be going over at least two to three chapters a day, Monday through Friday from 9:00 AM-4:00 PM. The content was crammed and we all had to make sure we were caught up on everything. With how the class was structured, I was reminded of my AP Psychology class my senior year of high school. I nearly failed that class in the first two months and yet I turned things around by graduation. Knowing what chapters were going to be covered the next day, I studied the material the night before and all I had to do was show up to class, open my notes, and listen to the lecture. Most of the content was terminology and that's all I needed to know. By the end of the year, I brought my grade up to an A average.

I decided to take this same approach for my real estate class, and it worked... almost. Every night, I would go home and read through the chapters and take notes. Even then, I found myself taking notes with the rest of the class sometimes because of newer laws or content I'd missed in my readings the night before.

The challenge lied within the depth of the content. I underestimated the amount of content each chapter had, and it was not consistent. Some chapters had 10 pages; others had 25 pages. My workflow was inconsistent and yet I had to keep going. Whatever it took to be aligned with the class and create the life I was destined to have; I was going to do it.

During this time, I noticed something different when I got home after class each day. I felt like I had a purpose. I hadn't had that feeling since college and it stuck with me. Even if I was just sitting in a classroom for a few hours a day, it was material that I wanted to learn. It was the lifestyle that I aligned myself with so much, that I didn't care how long it took me to finish my notes. I wanted this and I found that real estate was the vehicle for me to fulfill my passion.

CHAPTER 4

My BIG Why- 2014-2019

It was orientation week and the first-year students were settling into their new residence halls. I was an Orientation Leader (OL), and there was excitement throughout campus as new students unloaded their belongings with the help of their families. Along with the OLs, a move-in crew composed of upperclassmen helped the new students as well. I came back to campus a week before classes started to assist new students transition into college life while growing as a student leader myself through the OL program. Along with 60 other student leaders, I grew as a student-leader by understanding various student cultures on campus with increased self-awareness of my own identity within those cultures. I also developed teamwork skills through team building exercises and obstacle courses, and most importantly, created long-lasting connections with the other OLs. It was my second year as an OL and I looked forward to coming back to campus early for that one week. However, there was a dark cloud over my head.

I wasn't feeling one-hundred percent myself, and I was in a dark place because of a nasty break-up with my girlfriend at the time. To make the long story short, she cheated on me multiple times that summer and I forgave her like an idiot. Part of me wanted to move on and part of me didn't. It was a struggle to move on because at that point, we were together for five years. I started dating this girl at 15 years old. I was afraid of letting go because of all the time and energy invested into the relationship, even though it was clear she didn't have feelings for me anymore. Looking back, I was so stupid to have this girl mess me up so bad, and it was a huge waste of time being upset about it. I had to look forward and know that there is a WOMAN out there that will love me for who I am and will grow with me through thick and thin.

During a Carnival Night event for the first-year students, I was checking with the other OLs to see if they needed anything at their stations. We had a cotton candy station, games, dancing, catering and other stuff going on. The event was held in our student center, and the student leader office was on one side of the building. As I was headed toward the office to grab something, I noticed a familiar face. We locked eyes and I slowed my fast-walk to a slow-walk, and then stopped to talk to this beautiful woman. She was with Satin, a fellow OL, and I couldn't get over the fact that I knew of her from Chris, a mutual friend. I just didn't know her. I had to stop and say hello.

Asher: "Hey. You're that girl from Princeton. You're Chris's friend right?"

Beautiful Woman: (Laughs) "I'm not from Princeton, but yes, I'm friends with Chris."

Asher: "Got it. I just know that you're really smart. It's nice to meet you. Aren't you a sophomore? What are you doing on campus so early?"

Beautiful Woman: "I was part of the move-in crew, so I moved in early to help the new students."

Asher: "That's awesome. Are you enjoying the carnival?"

Beautiful Woman: "I just got here to meet with Satin. The event looks great."

Asher: "Well, thanks for coming by to help us out. Definitely grab some cotton candy, and enjoy the carnival."

Beautiful Woman: "I will. Thanks."

Asher: "Oh. What's your number? Maybe we can connect after OL week and get lunch sometime."

We exchanged numbers, and texted each other names to confirm. I remember her text vividly.

"Janay. It was a pleasure to meet you."

Two weeks after OL week was over, I didn't connect with Janay. As a matter of fact, I wasn't connecting with anyone. I was focused on boosting my self-esteem from the recent break-up. Deep down, I was depressed and my self-esteem was so low, I didn't feel worthy of having a lover one day. I even felt that I was not worthy of being successful in general, and I considered dropping out of school. The best way for me to cope with those feelings was to workout. I ran at least two miles a day, or until I threw up, and I would do hundreds of repetitions of push ups, squats, and crunches in the gym or in my room. Though it seemed like a healthy way to deal with the depression, I wasn't feeling any progress in my self-worth. I had to seek help, and I decided to receive counseling at the student wellness center. I found out during OL training that it was included in the tuition, so I figured it would help in some way. At the sametime, my Wealthy Dad started coaching me in personal development and I started doing affirmations as part of my already established Miracle Morning Routine. Between the counseling and affirmations, I started seeing a difference in how I felt and the days seemed to be brighter. I even started to connect with people more.

On a Thursday night, I went to an off-campus gathering with the other OLs. I didn't drink or anything, yet it was fun hanging out with the Leaders and catching up on how the first few weeks of school has been for us. I kept quiet about my depression though. During the event, I got a text from Janay saying hi. She asked what happened to connecting since the carnival, and I told her I was busy focusing on myself and classes. Throughout the event, we texted and as I was leaving the party, I asked if she wanted to meet up. We found out that we lived in the same residence hall on campus; Cedar Hall. It was a hall with suite-style rooms and you were deemed "lucky" if you snagged a room. My room was on the first floor and she lived on the second floor. When I got back from the party, I changed into my night clothes and I met with Janay on the second floor lounge.

From 11:00 PM to 5:00 AM, we just talked, laughed, and enjoyed each other's company. I found out that she was from Connecticut, and she played softball in high school. She was also a captain for her softball team and won a championship her senior year. For college, she was studying communications with a concentration in broadcast journalism. She also liked country music. At that time, I felt like I was the only person of color on campus that actually liked Luke Bryan and Darius Rucker, so I thought that was really neat. I also learned that her father was a pastor and their church was in Newark. Her family has been going to church in New Jersey her whole life and their church was only ten minutes away from my house back home. I couldn't believe her family did that two hour, round trip ride every week for so many years. I also couldn't believe that this beautiful woman was only a stone-throws away from my house on the weekends this whole time. During our conversation, I truly felt happy and it was like we were meant to meet each other. I didn't want to jump to conclusions though. I wanted to build this friendship organically and see where it goes. I also needed more time before I started getting into an exclusive relationship again. After we called it a night, I went to bed with renewed energy in my heart. I slept in and missed my 9:00 AM communications class, which was my only class on Fridays. I didn't care though because I was looking forward to seeing her again.

In October 2014, we eventually made it official and the rest was history. It seemed like I was rushing into a new relationship yet I realized that I didn't need to waste anymore time dwelling on what could have been with the other girl. I knew my worth, and I knew I deserved better.

During Thanksgiving break that same year, I introduced Janay to my mom and at first glance, she got excited to meet Janay, and she's already welcoming her into the family. Then during our winter break, I officially met her parents at their home in Connecticut for dinner. I was also introduced to their dog, Kaleb, their black labrador.

During dinner, I remember her father jokingly asked me, "So why do you like my daughter?"

I remember saying something amongst the lines of, "Well, she is an incredible young woman that makes me feel happy and joyful when I'm with her and she actually pulled me out of a dark place when we started to connect. I cherish her very much."

Not sure if that helped with my candidacy, yet he seemed satisfied with the answer.

As the years went by, we went to Penn State Football games and other sports events, made memories on campus, traveled home together, started going to church together, graduated college, got jobs, and eventually, in 2018, I popped the question in New York City. At the time, she was working in Upstate New York and I was working in New Jersey. She came back home for her birthday weekend and I wanted her to go back with a ring on her finger. It was also our fourth year anniversary that following Monday, so it was great timing.

After church, I drove us to the city, having her think we were going to see *Wicked on Broadway*. Little did she know that I would be bringing us near the World Trade Center (WTC) to propose. I planned everything the month before, including getting the moment captured with Malcolm, her brother-in-law, as the photographer. Malcolm has a photography business as his side-hustle and his work is incredible. I wanted him to capture our moment. He worked in the city for his full-time job and his shift was over before church service was out, so everything lined up. I wanted the WTC tower to be the background and I found a Marriott hotel that had a great view of the tower from a restaurant terrace. All in all, the proposal was successful and I took her to a celebratory dinner at Morton's Steakhouse before taking her back home.

I'm not sure how much I can express my love for Janay. She truly was a huge part of my success in college and there's no doubt, she'll be a bigger contribution in my success in life as a wife. When I started my personal development in college, my Wealthy Dad gave me an exercise in finding the right woman for me. He told me to list everything I desired in a woman, not just physically, but in terms of her character. I wanted someone smart, intelligent, caring, loyal, faith-based, fun, adventurous, and always striving to be better in life. I didn't want an average woman. I desired a helpmate. I desired a woman that would push me to evolve into a stronger man everyday. Yet, before that woman appeared in my life, I had to become all of that myself, and ultimately, I had to love myself. I had to love the person I was then and love the person I was striving to become. On God's timing, Janay is everything I asked for and more, and I want to give her the world.

I knew that real estate was the vehicle that would drive me to do just that. I didn't have time to dwell on losing my job. I had to focus on what i've been given now and make the best out of it. Janay is my **BIG WHY** that will pull all my other "whys" and I was ready to take advantage of the opportunity that God has placed before me. I will marry my softball player queen.

CHAPTER 5

Traveling the Journey Together-
July 11, 2019

When I signed up for the class, I made the decision based on my enthusiasm, passion, and excitement. I made the choice based on MY feelings. What I failed to do was consider the impact that my decision would have on others, particularly my loved ones. I'm usually the type of person that doesn't care about what others think of me and yet part of my determination to get things done was due to my obligation to make my family proud and to give the world to my fiancé. I didn't tell her about the class until two days later.

When I first got into real estate investing, I was so excited about it that I had no idea what to do with myself or the actual concept itself. I remember telling Janay what I was looking to do, and she was NOT for it. In her defense, I was not explaining it thoroughly and it came out of nowhere. I even asked her to start looking for homes for me to call and put deals together, without giving any context and just saying "I'm doing real estate investing and I need to talk to as many homeowners as I can to make this work". Sometimes, we get excited about an idea because we see the potential in what it can bring to our lives. However, some people wouldn't want any part of it, and there are a few reasons for that:

- They have little to no interest in what you're doing
- The idea seems so crazy and is deemed "unrealistic"
- They do not know enough about the concept
- They have limited belief in themselves and do what they can to project that limiting belief onto you

In this case, I didn't give a lot of context and wasn't as confident in explaining real estate investing thoroughly to Janay. I just saw something I liked, said yes, and jumped. So, when I told Janay about the real estate class, she was upset because I didn't tell her and felt that I'd left her out of certain life-altering decisions. At first, I was upset because she was upset, and I felt that she was looking to steer me out of real estate for good. The reality was that I was selfish in not sharing what getting a license would do for me and how it would set me up in finding a job. At this point in our relationship, it was common sense to share **ANYTHING AND EVERYTHING** to each other, regardless of how we may react to the news. Eventually, we both talked it through, and everything was well. I explained how the license could open opportunities for me as an operations associate, plus making extra money selling homes part-time. From there, she was very supportive in making sure I was getting my notes done and understood the amount of focus I needed to pass my test.

If you want your significant other to stick around for the long-term, **tell them everything.** If you want your partner to be there when times are good, you better tell them everything when times are bad. They always say, *if you want to go fast, go alone. If you want to go far, go with others.*

I knew I wanted to go far in life and the journey is more enjoyable because I have a strong, godly woman by my side. This wasn't just my journey; it was our journey.

CHAPTER **6**

Having Fun with the Grind

Aside from the insane number of hours dedicated to earning my real estate license, I also set time to relax and have playtime. Anyone who knows me knows I'm not as big on video games now, compared to my high school days, and yet I still have a knack of playing Call of Duty an hour a day for a break. I would also play video games with my younger brother, Aaron, who had serious gaming skills. I also spent my free time going to the movies in the middle of the afternoon or late at night. I had to get out of the house and let the study material settle in my mind. Going to the movies was a great way for me to take a break and have somewhat of a social life. Early in the summer, I bought a subscription to a monthly movie membership that allowed me to see three showings a week for "free". Sometimes, I would take my mom or my brother if they wanted to come and just pay for their tickets. I also used the movie subscription to stay up until Janay finished work. At that time, she was working the evening news, and since her contract was almost over, she spent extra time after her shift to put her demo reel together for her interviews. I wanted to make sure she got home safe.

To be honest, I wasn't a big fan of going to the movies until *Marvel Studios' Black Panther* movie came out in 2018. That was the movie that got me to go out and pay for a ticket in a long time. I loved the movie so much, I saw it *nine* times in every movie format possible, including 3D- and 3D sucks!

Even though I had a destination in my mind, I also had to remember how to enjoy the journey. When we endeavor on long trips, we tend to make a pit stop or two to refuel on gas, food, and sleep.

While I was working toward my real estate license, I had to remind myself of a saying my Wealthy Father once told me growing up: **"All work and no play makes Jack a dull boy. All play and no work makes Jack a dumb boy."**

I had to balance my time between working and relaxing. Life is not all about the work we do day-to-day. The key to an extraordinary life is to enjoy the small moments. For me, those moments included hanging out with my family, catching up with Janay, and watching *John Wick 3* all summer long in Dolby Atmos, the best surround sound technology anyone can ever experience in theatres, in my opinion. I even had a full-day of paintball with Aaron and Malcolm. It was these moments that reminded me of why I was working toward my goal of being in real estate and it was those moments that kept me human.

CHAPTER 7

All Roads Lead to the Centennial-July 25, 2019

I made it to the last week of the class and I was proud to have done so. I befriended a few classmates that wanted to connect for study sessions for the school test at the end of the week and yet I wouldn't be able to join. That Thursday, I was set to fly out to Greensboro, North Carolina, with Janay, for our church's 100th Convocation. It was a big deal and we'd planned on going since the location of the Centennial was announced months ago. At first, I was hesitant to keep the plan because of the lack of income, and yet I had saved enough to pay for my portion of the flight, car rental, hotel, and spending money. Besides, not going to the event would mean missing out on the blessings and miracles that may come my way.

Janay and I flew down to Charlotte from Newark that Thursday morning. When we arrived, we had to pick up our rental car to drive an hour and fifteen minutes to Greensboro. When we got in line for pick up, I received a scary text. My mom sent me a text saying she received a letter in the mail from the New Jersey Motor Vehicle Commission regarding a suspension. Earlier in the summer, I found out that my driver's license was suspended because of an unpaid New York State speeding ticket from late 2017. The crazy part was that the suspension was in effect since January 2019; I had been driving around town to town, crossing state lines for over nine months illegally. I never got a notice about the suspension and if I did, I can't explain what happened to them. For a week, I went back and forth to the New Jersey Motor Vehicle office to renew my license that was set to expire in August. Eventually, I was able to lift the suspension and get my renewed license before the Centennial trip. When I looked at my mothers message, I thought, "what do I do?"

Part of me didn't want to believe it was real. It may have been a delayed letter from before or perhaps my mom misread it. I googled what would happen if the person who rented a car had an expired license and had another person with them. Some answers showed there was no chance of getting the rental at all as they run a background check on driver history on the spot or the other person would have their information on file and be able to take the rental. Focusing on that possibility, I proceeded to the front desk and I gave my identification to the clerk. He took a long time looking at his screen and checking my license and looking at the screen again. He then called over a co-worker and pointed at the screen as they whispered something to each other.

After about five minutes of waiting, the clerk said, "Okay Mr. Carr. Thanks for your patience. We're just checking on the available cars for your order. Would you also like to purchase an insurance package for your rental?"

"YES!" I said through a sigh of relief.

We got our keys to the rental, headed up to the parking deck, and saw a beautiful, massive black Ford Taurus as our ride for the weekend. Once we'd packed the car, we set Google Maps to the Centennial and hit the road. I was still in shock of getting through the rental check-in. I was very uncertain of the outcome and still questioned the true status of my license (I checked later that night. The letter confirmed my suspension was lifted and I was cleared to drive again. I was good!). The one thing I was certain of while I was driving was that I was meant to be at that conference. This was my time to seek the answers I needed and to be prepared for the miracles, signs, and wonders that God will provide for me moving forward. This was my winning season!

CHAPTER 8

Holy Clarity- July 27, 2019

Throughout the weekend, I had the opportunity to attend numerous services, see vendors that served the church, and catch up with friends and acquaintances from all over the country. Experiencing Greensboro was fun as well. While Janay stayed at the main hotel with her parents, I had the rental car and stayed at a Marriott 10 minutes away from the event. I shared a room with Ebonee, Janay's older sister, and Malcolm, so we could minimize costs for the trip. During the first two nights, I stayed up to take notes and study for the real estate chapters I was missing that week. I was slated to take the school exam as soon as I returned home. After studying each night, I would take a drive to a nearby Sheetz and grab a late-night snack with Malcolm. A trip to Sheetz was always a win in my book. The rest of the convention was packed with things to do, including concerts. I even got the opportunity to see John P. Key perform a Live concert for free with Janay and the family. It was a blast. The man even gave an 85-year-old missionary nearly $1,000 in cash just because he wanted to bless someone.

During a youth concert they held, the choir was singing beautifully and at one point, everything just shifted. At the high point of a song, the room just burst into prayer, people were speaking in tongues and everyone was giving themselves to God. For me, I was thinking of everything that had happened so far in 2019 and I couldn't stop thinking about the goodness that God had provided me with. Despite the circumstances of being broke, I had a roof over my head, I had food to eat, I had clothes on my back, I had friends that cared about me, I had a mother and brother that loves me, I had a church I could go to, and I had a woman that chose to love me through everything. I was grateful for the opportunity to work on myself with the free time I had and become the person God needed me to be. It may have seemed like I didn't have a lot and yet I did have enough to keep going in life. This wave of gratitude hit me hard and I just started crying tears of joy. This was the moment I just let all my burdens go and gave glory to God.

That was the moment I needed to confirm that everything was going to be alright. Amid working toward a goal, sometimes we forget the little things that helped us get far on the journey to success. It's easy to think about the negative and yet it's easy to give credit to the positive, too. It didn't matter how much money I had in my bank account; I knew I was going to be a millionaire someday- it was just a matter of time. This was just all part of a bigger story I didn't know I was writing for. When we change the way we look at things, the things we look at change. My wallet may have been near empty and yet my faith was full of grace, love, and mercy. A miracle was coming my way.

CHAPTER 9

The Knocking on the Door Gets Louder- August 16, 2019

Because of the Centennial trip, my real estate instructor told me that I needed to attend two more classes to be eligible to take the test. I was able to make up the missed classes through sitting in night sessions taught by another instructor. After that, I was scheduled to take the test.

I studied like a crazy person every night. I didn't even go to the movies for my usual showings. This test was my make or break to get to the national test. I had to sacrifice a little, so I could acquire a lot. The day of the test came, and I was ready to conquer it.

I arrived at the school 30 minutes early. I looked at my notes for one last run-through, then said my affirmations, my usual priming routine. Every morning, I read a list of affirmations that speak victory into my day and it helps boost my confidence in whatever I aim to do for the day. Sometimes, I read my affirmations again for special occasions, such as life-changing exams. This was my way of prayer. When it comes to taking tests, I don't recall being nervous or anxious during my college years, or even high school years. However, this was different, and I had plenty of reasons to be nervous. My classmate, Mike, took his test while I was in Greensboro and he told me exactly what to study. He said it was tough, even though he passed it on the first go.

Ten minutes before the test started, I walked to the classroom and signed in. I sat at a desk and my instructor waited for another student to sign in before we began. A few minutes later, I was handed the test and it was go-time. Over 110 questions to answer in 120 minutes. I had to work fast and buffer enough time to read through the test at least three times- and I did just that. During the second read through, I took the time to read the questions and made sure the answers lined up with them.

With 30 minutes left and having read through the test FOUR times, I decided to submit my test and pray for the best. The instructor told me she would grade it ASAP and email the results to me later that day. I walked back to my car and took a big breather. I was done for now and could rest. I wasn't sure what I wanted to do, so I sat in the car for a few minutes and looked at my phone. I was looking through the Zillow alerts I had set up for myself and I was looking at homes in Alpine, New Jersey. Then, I had an idea for myself. When I passed the school test, I was going to take a trip to Alpine and drive-by the amazing homes to see them in person. Just like any other test, this one set the tone for the rest of the day and I couldn't wait to see my results.

CHAPTER **10**

Driving By Possibilities-
August 16, 2019

As I lounged on the sofa when I got home, I was going through my email for job applications when I received a notification; it was from the real estate school. The results were in! Right away, I saw my result in the subject line when I was scrolling to it and it read, *Congratulations on Passing Final School Test.* I PASSED!

The rest of the email read, *Hi Asher, Congratulations on passing the Final School Exam. You had 20 wrong answers.*

Even though I wasn't happy with the number of wrong answers, I was still elated about passing. Who doesn't love the feeling of getting through a test and earning a good grade? All I had to do was take the test one more time at a national testing center to get the license. Until then, I was going to celebrate. As I promised to myself, I headed to Alpine, New Jersey with a Starbucks chai latte by my side to get a preview of what my future will hold.

From home, it took about 45 minutes to get to Alpine. The roads were a little tough to navigate as the roadway toward the township felt as if it was hidden from the rest of the roads coming off the George Washington Bridge exit. As I was driving down the parkway, there was a spectacular view of the Hudson River. It was a gorgeous sunny day, and the sun was shining off the water. The exit was approaching, and I was officially in Alpine. My first impression of the town upon seeing the welcome sign was that it was in the middle of nowhere. I didn't set a specific address to see, so I pulled over and looked at my recent Zillow listings in the area. I entered a property address that was only five minutes away and headed there. As I drove, I saw a massive gate with a long driveway behind it. It was the $32,000,000 house my Wealthy Dad and I saw online. The driveway to a home was incredible and the mansion looked more like a convention center. The route to the house I was viewing was very scenic. This house was located on top of a hill. Not sure how people would be able to deal with that during the winter.

Finally, I made it to the top, and there it was- Stone Manor. Per the listing description:

This palatial, stone manor with slate roof sits on 2 acres of a quiet, cul-de-sac street in one of the most sought-

after zip codes in the United States. From the basement to the third floor, this home was designed and built with entertaining in mind. The first floor includes a grand kitchen with breakfast room and butler's pantry, music room, dining room, and great room with a wine bar and guest suite. 5-bedroom suites including Master with his/her bathrooms and closet finish out the second floor. The third floor provides additional living space. Lower level with theatre, spa with jacuzzi and fireplace, gym, massage room, billiard room with bar, and guest suite. The garage can accommodate up to 6 cars. Elevator to all four floors. Pre-wired for smart home capabilities. Large outdoor entertainment area in rear yard with fireplace, pool, and spa. From the ultimate Master Bedroom closet to relaxing in your very own 5-star spa, this home fits the wants of even the most discerning buyer.

It was a sight to see. I took a few pictures as a keepsake. There was a major difference between viewing a home virtually and viewing it physically, even if it was just the exterior. I felt a strong vibe coming off the mansion that I'd never felt before, and it felt right. Taking a gander at the mansion made me realize what's possible and what I desired in a home. Although, I wouldn't get a mansion for myself and indulge in the incredible amenities they come with. It takes two to build an empire and I wanted that for Janay and me. The idea of owning a home of that caliber set the standard of how I wanted to live, and it took a mindset shift to accomplish such a goal.

If I desired to give Janay the whole world, I had to change how I operated in mine.

I would also buy a family mansion for my mother and Janay's parents to live in. Both sides would have their own wing of the home, outfitted with what they needed to live comfortably. They could get away from the stresses of the world with the uses of the pool, spa, movie theatre, and everything else. They wouldn't have to worry about paying the mortgage or anything else. Just move in and relax. This dream would later morph into a family compound idea, where everyone would have their own home and amenities.

Ever since I got into entrepreneurship and understood the possibilities in all aspects of life, I've made it a point to give back to my parents, especially my mother. She's been through hell and high-water taking care of me and my brother. She had to navigate America on her own as she left her family back in the Philippines, seeking opportunities to live the American Dream. Although I don't know every single detail of her journey, I know that she deserves to be rewarded for providing for the family. I wasn't in the ideal situation at 25 years old and yet she still loved me and always prayed for me, and I knew I was going to fulfill my goals in giving back to her.

The same goes for my future parent in-laws. They could've cut me out of their lives and convinced Janay to leave me for not having a job amid wedding planning. They could've turned the other cheek and acted as if I never existed. However, they loved me unemployed as much as they loved me as a full-time financial analyst. There was never a negative word spoken; only positive affirmation. Their support during this time truly meant the world to me and what way to show them my love and appreciation for them than to give an open door to a future home.

Most of all, I wanted to provide for the love of my life. She didn't have to stick with me during this journey and yet she stayed loyal and faithful since day one. I wasn't aloof to the fact that this unemployment situation was hurting her and the uncertainty it comes with. However, she gave me the opportunity to go after what I desired and that was all I could ask for. I'm going to give her the world and we are going to thrive through this together.

For the next hour and a half, I drove through Alpine and the surrounding towns to look at other incredible houses and mansions. Feeding my mind with what I desired expanded my vision to give back to my family and more. I would leave that town with more inspiration and motivation than ever before and there was not a damn thing that was going to stop me from achieving greatness. My breakthrough was coming, and I was just one test away.

CHAPTER 11

Licensed to Be a Millionaire-
September 3, 2019

After the state received my clearance to take the national exam from the real estate school, I scheduled an 8:30 AM session before spots were booked in the month of August. This would be marked as the day I would be licensed to become a millionaire! Leading up to the test, I had to find a way of studying the right material without breaking the bank. I had maxed out the practice test in the school workbook and the free tests on the internet could only help so much. I had to look for a state-specific book that also had national material. I decided to drive to Livingston Mall and check out Barnes and Noble. Fortunately, there were few copies of Barons Real Estate Test Booklets available. To save myself some money and sanity, I decided to take the test at the bookstore every day until test day. I brought my bookbag, pens and a notebook to the store, grabbed the study booklet, and sat down in the Starbucks café. When I took the practice test, I timed myself and wrote down my answers in the notebook as I went. I practiced the same way I did for the school test; went through the whole thing once, and then read through another two times to make sure I was confident in my answers. Most of the time, I finished early with an average of 30 minutes left. For the grades, I wasn't doing too bad. I scored 85% on average and that was more than enough to pass. By the time August 21st rolled around, I was ready to conquer the test.

On the morning of the test, I left my house around 7:15 AM. The testing center was in Parsippany and I would get there in 15 minutes. In 2016, I took my life insurance tests at this testing facility, so I was familiar with the location. I went through my notes for one last time, said my affirmations, and walked into the building at 8:10 AM.

When I got to the test room, I walked in and said good morning to the moderator. She told me to take a seat while we waited for the other applicants to show up. The room looked the same as before. Lockers were available for us to store our personal belongings away, the desk of the moderator was in the middle of the room, and behind that desk was another room full of computer desks where the actual test was held. Eventually, everyone showed up and the sign-in process began. Signing in seemed like going through the CIA. The moderator had to read a set of rules to everyone, then call us individually and confirm our ID, which test we were taking, and all this other stuff. As soon as she assigned me to my computer, I put my stuff into the locker, and marched toward the door to the computer room and took my seat at computer seven. IT WAS GO TIME!

I signed into my test, answered a few practice questions, and officially launched the exam. Everything I had worked for led up to this moment. One-hundred and ten questions in 120 minutes and I was on fire. I answered each question in under a minute. I skipped the math-related questions for later and picked the best answers that would get me to my goal of being licensed in real estate.

I had 20 minutes left and I was anxious to submit the test for grading. I ran through the test four times and made all the changes I had to. There was no reason to sit there any longer and get more anxious; I was ready to go. I submitted my full test, filled out a feedback section, and then walked out to the moderator for my final grade. She asked how I felt about it and I answered, "I'm feeling pretty good". As she was pulling up my results, her smile slowly turned into a frown. "I'm sorry, Hun. It seems that you didn't pass. You missed it by eight questions."

I just shut down and felt my heart racing as if I were getting in trouble by my mom or Janay for doing something stupid. I couldn't believe it. The moderator gave me a breakdown of my test and it showed where I needed improvement. I would have to take this test again, just like the insurance tests. I walked out feeling defeated and angry. All summer, I drove back and forth to Barnes and Noble every day and dedicated my whole summer learning about the basics of being an agent. I wasn't sure if I was ready for this. I started to consider looking into contract positions in finance again. I was losing time in making this wedding happen and I needed money fast.

I then realized that I couldn't go back to where I started; I couldn't give up so easily. Becoming a financial analyst couldn't be an option anymore. I'm reminded of a story in the Bible about Lot being told by Angels to leave the cities of Sodom and Gomorrah because they would be destroyed due to the great amount of sin committed by its people.

As the Angels commanded Lot to leave the city with his wife and kids, Genesis 19:17 NIV says, "Flee for your lives! **Don't look back**, and don't stop anywhere in the plain! Flee to the mountains or you will be swept away!"

By the time Lot and his family reached safety from Sodom and Gomorrah in verse 26, Lot's wife looked back and turned into a pillar of salt. From how I see it, being let go from my finance job is the equivalent to the destruction of Sodom and Gomorrah. Sitting at a desk feeling unfulfilled, being surrounded by mediocrity, and reluctantly attending happy hours with co-workers who talked about nothing purposeful was the environment I needed to get away from. I couldn't look back and stay stuck with getting comfortable with the wrong people. I needed to grow. I needed to keep my eyes on the mountains and never look back.

Tony Robbins once said, "If you are going to take the island, you **burn the boat.**"

I decided to burn that boat when I signed up for real estate school. I had to take the island of promise and I wasn't going to let eight questions stop me from reaching my destiny.

A few days later, I signed up for a new test date for September 3rd, 2019 at 10:00 AM in New Providence, NJ. I studied ten times harder leading up to test day and got smarter in answering the questions on the practice exams. Even with the same anxieties as the previous test, I had faith in myself that I was going to pass this test. This time, on test day, I decided to walk in earlier and the moderator didn't wait for a big group to start the process. She checked me in ASAP and got me into the computer lab within a few minutes. I got to my computer, and it was go-time. As I was going through the test, it seemed that I was moving quicker than the last test and yet I had a stream of confidence that wasn't there before. I wasn't doing anything differently, except for one thing. I decided to run the clock out on the exam. I went through that test five times and barely made changes after the second run through. As soon as that clock ran out, I sat at the front desk for my results.

"How did you do?" the moderator asked.

"I think I did alright," I replied. I was looking down at my shoes and clutching my hands together as I waited for the results.

A few moments went by and the moderator whispered, "It's alright. I think you passed."

I looked up at her with a slight grin replying, "No way."

She nodded her head and printed my certificate of completion.

"Congratulations, Mr. Carr." She then explained the next steps in getting the form processed with the state, along with setting up an appointment to get fingerprinted.

I said thank you to her, grabbed my belongings, and marched out to my car.

I FREAKING DID IT! I screamed in my car with joy. I'd achieved my biggest goal of the summer, becoming a licensed real estate agent. I texted Janay and she was happy for me. She knew how much that test meant to me and it was an incredible feeling. It was that day when I was licensed to be a millionaire.

CHAPTER **12**

Finding My Place in Real Estate- September 4, 2019

Now that I have my license, I was more confident in applying to real estate positions and felt like the job hunt wouldn't be as difficult. The only reason why I pursued a real estate license was to have insight into what a real estate agent experienced and how I could contribute to their business from an administrative level. Yes, I was aware that I could sell real estate for myself and make extra money, it just wasn't my focus at the time. I wasn't in the position to be a commission-only worker. I needed a salary to get back on my feet again. One of my favorite quotes about working full-time while having a side hustle is from the successful late business philosopher, Jim Rohn.

Mr. Rohn always emphasized, "Work full-time on your job and part-time on your fortune."

I was looking for that full-time job in real estate operations, so I could be around the people and resources that could help me build my fortune.

Jim also said, "Service to many leads to greatness."

I'm not aiming for accolades or medals. I just wanted to serve others that thought like me and help them be better at what they do. I didn't know how that was going to look and yet I knew I was going to make it happen.

When I took the real estate class, the instructor told us that we had the freedom of placing our license with any firm upon completion of licensure. There were many big-name companies in real estate I could've applied to and yet the only one I had my heart set on was Keller Williams Realty International (KWRI). In one of my masterminds, I was connected to highly successful individuals, many of them earning their riches through real estate as investors and agents. The platform that 99 percent of them leveraged to reach their success was Keller Williams.

Kami, a close friend of mine I met through the group, found her breakthrough as a KW agent and we connected through sharing similar goals. During that time, she launched the Keller Williams Young Professionals (KWYP) Twin Cities Chapter in Minnesota. Then, she turned her primary home into a rental property and started to build her real estate investment portfolio.

She was making things happen in her life through real estate at the age of 26 and I wanted to follow suit. The only question was how and when. Every KW affiliate I met had incredible things to say about the company and had a sense of fulfillment and purpose in their life. When I started to do research on the company, their mission statement aligned with what I was seeking in life:

> *To build careers worth having,*
> *businesses worth owning, lives*
> *worth living, experiences worth*
> *giving, and legacies worth leaving.*

However, the icing on the cake for me was when I read their values: *God, family, then business.*

This was the first time I'd seen a company even mention the word "God" in their company overview and the order of those values was what led me to do whatever it took to join the brand.

In the month of September, I interviewed at two KW offices in Livingston and Montclair. The Livingston interview was for an Executive Assistant position and I interviewed with the Team Leader there. She even invited me for a training session with some of the agents later that day. Unfortunately, nothing came out of that interview. Then I interviewed at an office in Montclair. That interview was for placing my license there and I wanted to learn the possibilities that the team would bring me. As stated before, I was looking for a full-time position and the Team Leader for that office did what she could to connect me with such positions. However, nothing came out of there as well.

After a while, it seemed that finding my place in real estate was becoming more difficult. Either I was overqualified, too new, or they didn't want me at all. I started to feel defeated. Also, I didn't have a lot of cash left to drive around or do anything. I was borderline broke, and I didn't know what to do. I spent a chunk of my last dollars on the real estate exams while borrowing some money from my mom just to get by. I started to panic, and I lost sight of what was possible. I didn't understand why no one was taking me seriously in my interviews in NJ or NYC. What else did I need to stand out and how could I finance myself to get through this?

CHAPTER **13**

Running on Empty Tolls- September 5, 2019

Interviewing for KW was exciting and yet there was still a sense of uncertainty about where I would end up. Even with numerous positions popping up at different locations, one position was common amongst the offices: Market Center Administrator (MCA). This position was what I was striving for since I started my search in KW. At a high level, the MCA was in charge of the financial accounting of a KW office and processed the payments of commission checks. They also had to report the office financials to HQ every month, so the magnitude of an MCA was huge. Despite the heavy math involved, I was willing and able to take on such a position and I applied for every MCA position that was out there. One office in particular took interest in me in New York.

While I was mowing the church lawn in late June, I received a call from Deeon, a Team Leader from a

KW office in the Bronx. He was responding to my application for MCA and wanted to meet with me to talk more about the position. We met two days before the Fourth of July and the interview went well. Although he was impressed with my resume, his one concern was the time gaps between my previous positions. I explained that a few of them were contracts, while the others were full-time with a story explaining my departures.

He then asked, "Why do you think this would be a concern for me?"

I answered, "Well sir, a new hire's potential lies in their loyalty and that they are an investment in the eyes of leadership."

He strongly agreed with me and emphasized the investment piece of a new hire. He didn't want to regret putting in the time and money into someone that wouldn't make a substantial return to the business with the type of track record I had. I was certain that I wouldn't be invited back to another interview as soon as he said that.

He then continued, "I like you a lot, Asher. You have strong potential for this role, but I need to get a deeper understanding of who you really are. I'm going to have you take a KPA."

"I do have a copy of my KPA from May if you would like?" I said.

"That's okay. I would like an updated one. It should be the same if anything. Do you have time to take it now?"

I agreed to take the test and he set up a KPA assessment in the conference room across from us. The Keller Personality Assessment (KPA) is what potential hires take in KW and outlines the best positions one should consider. I took my first KPA when I was working with my job coach, Steve, back in May. He and his wife were both KW agents and ran a talent acquisition business as well. Based on my first results, Steve agreed that I had the personality and work ethic to work in management and sales. Through that first assessment, we determined that the MCA position would be a great starting position for me in real estate.

The KPA took about 45 minutes to complete and taking it a second time was just as fun as the first. After I submitted my test, I walked over to Deeon's office and we went over my results. We spent some time going over each part of the test and what it had to say about certain criterias of my personality. For the most part, everything checked out, and Deeon decided to push me through the next round in the interview process.

Deeon explained that I would have to take a small accounting test to get a baseline idea of what that skillset looked like. I would also have to send him my personal and professional goals that I would like to achieve in real estate. Based on the accounting results, I would be invited back for a final group interview with his market center staff. I agreed to move forward, and then headed back home with confidence and joy, knowing that I was still in the game.

A week later, I received the accounting test and went to Staples to print it out and completed the test at the store. It took an hour to go through. Fortunately, the accounting principles I needed to demonstrate were basic enough for me to recall from my accounting classes in college. I had to take the class twice; once for general accounting every business major needed- and most of us barely passed, and the second time specifically for entrepreneurship. I felt pretty good about my results and I scanned my test to Deeon as soon as I could. All I had to do was wait.

I waited two more weeks until I heard from Deeon. When we spoke on the phone, Deeon said his leadership was impressed with my test results and needed some extra information for the next steps. It was more for background check purposes and paperwork he needed to fill out. He told me he would get back to me ASAP to schedule the group interview. I wouldn't hear from Deeon until a week after the Centennial. When I was on the road fueling up for gas, he called me and explained that he didn't get back to me until then because there was a concern about compensation. The market center had a cap for the MCA position, which was slightly lower than what it usually pays. He was unsure of how to present a potential offer to me when the salary would be lower than expected and he was working to fight for the expected pay.

At that point, I didn't even worry about the money. I just knew that whatever I would get paid as an employee would be better than not getting paid at all. I was driving around with little to no money on my EZ-Pass all summer and I only took the hit on the account if the drive was worth it for job interviews. When I first met with Deeon, my EZ-Pass had $10 and I had to cross the George Washington Bridge to get to the office, which was a $15 toll. I was already doing what it took to get this far in an interview, and I wasn't in a position to request for higher pay.

I told Deeon I was willing to accept the lower salary and he was relieved of my choice. From there, he was able to schedule the group interview in mid-August, after a company conference in Texas. On the day, I drove to the office with no money on my EZ Pass. I knew that I was going to get a violation notice eventually and yet I had to do what it took to get through this interview process. Overall, the interview went well. The group seemed to like me and allowed me to go through my resume in depth. After the interview, Deeon told me he'd have an answer by next week. I felt like a winner leaving that interview.

A week went by and I was expecting a call from Deeon that Thursday morning. I was anxious about what he would say and yet I felt confident in getting the position. The extra steps and meetings Deeon had to put us through proved otherwise. At 11:00 AM, I received the call and Deeon told me the result:

"I had a meeting with my boss this morning and advocated strongly for you. But ultimately, the commute was the breaking point. They told me they would like to have someone with NY roots and have me focus my search closer to home."

As soon as I heard that, my heart just broke. I didn't know what to say and I felt that all the miles and (lack of) tolls I paid for were wasted.

He continued, "For the record man, I wanted to bring you in. You had everything we needed for the position but the regional leadership said otherwise. I know this was an exhaustive process and I appreciate you seeing it through. But again, I think you have everything that KW represents, and you are headed in the right direction. If you are still considering a job within KW, let me know and I'll put in a strong recommendation for you. I know you're going to get in and once you're in, you're in."

I thanked Deeon for his time and the opportunity. Knowing that I had a recommendation from someone in leadership was the best thing to come out of the whole experience. I hung up the phone and took a moment to accept the rejection. I knew from the beginning of the interview that it was going to be tough and yet getting the "no" was something I hadn't expected. However, Deeon did share something with me when we met that helped me manage my emotions upon receiving the news.

When it comes to building a strong team, their motto is: *Hire Slow. Fire Fast.*

Immediately, I respected the way the interview would play out and all I had to do was to give my all.

After a while, I didn't see this as a loss; this was a win in knowing that another team would be able to leverage my talents at a high level and the return on investment would be ten-fold. The only question was: When?

CHAPTER **14**

Cashing In Defeat-
September 28, 2019

It was a brisk morning in Norwalk, Connecticut and I was waiting in the car for one of the silliest yet awesome people I've gotten to know over the last few years, Ebonee, Janay's older sister. When I first started dating Janay, Ebonee was just as welcoming as their parents and yet she knew when to throw down when needed. We connected over her pronunciation of the opening lines to *The Circle of Life* from *The Lion King*. It was so weird yet hilarious. We connected so well that she and Malcolm would open their doors to me whenever I was in the area for real estate investment networking events. I drove up the night before to ride with Ebonee to Elmira, NY for Janay's birthday weekend. Ebonee and I left at the crack of dawn, picked up their older brother, Karlton, from his apartment, got some donuts and coffee from Donut Delight, and trekked for the seven-hour trip. During the ride, Ebonee and I got to share personal stories with each other dating back to our college days and childhood. Although we had already established a solid connection, that was the first time we actually shared deep stories to each other without feeling embarrassed or shameful. However, I didn't tell her about my job search. I wasn't ready to say anything to anyone yet. I always wanted a sister and she would be a great future sister-in-law if I can make this wedding happen. Karlton was also a great future brother-in-law. He works in the restaurant industry as a manager, and I don't get to see him often. When we do connect, it's organic and we talk about business and whatever was on our minds at the moment. This time, he was asleep throughout the whole ride, recovering from his late-shift at work. Overall, I was in the presence of good people and my future in-laws.

As we were approaching town, I had this odd feeling inside me knowing that I was traveling with very little money. I even booked a hotel for some of the family and myself and I didn't know how I was going to pay for it. I nearly finished the last check from the last job, and it was embarrassing, even though no one in the family knew, except Janay's parents and my mother.

When we got to Elmira, Ebonee, Karlton, and I got some rest at Janay's apartment before all four of us headed to Ithaca for the afternoon. There was a festival going on that we weren't aware of, so we took advantage of that and enjoyed ourselves. Knowing what little cash I had, approximately $20 in cash and another $40 in the bank, I only spent money on Janay or if I was super hungry.

Thank God for the family though because I didn't have to worry too much about expenses during that weekend. When I booked a hotel room for Mark and Carolina, Janay's older brother and sister-in-law, Mark was kind enough to cover my room for the night as well. Little did I know that he knew about my situation, which was ok because he is my Youth Pastor. Outside of church, we are very similar in many ways and he's an overall incredible guy to be around. After settling into the hotel room, I pulled an all-nighter finishing up Janay's birthday gift and adding the final touches. At some point, I took a break to text Janay before she went to sleep, and I told her about my money situation. She asked about applying for unemployment and I suddenly remembered something.

When I was let go, the final paperwork included an unemployment form. I had the option to file for unemployment and receive a weekly check until I found a full-time job again. At the time, filing for unemployment was a sign of defeat for me. I didn't want to give in to the idea that I had no job. I had enough money during that time, and I was secure in that. On the other hand, I saw that the form was a blessing. My last job didn't have to give me unemployment. I'm not sure if it's against the law to not provide the unemployment benefits and yet I felt like they didn't want to let me go drowning. The unemployment form was what I needed, and I had to put my pride to the side and follow-through. This is my livelihood I was talking about. I decided to create my unemployment account the next day, and file for the coming week.

The next day, we attended a church service nearby, and then we went to a hiking trail for most of the day. In hindsight, the hike was something I needed, being one with nature and appreciating the little things. With everything happening back home, I had to get away to slow things down. Even when I was working, it was a challenge to simply relax and enjoy time with my loved ones. I've walked the hiking trail with Janay before on a previous visit and yet doing it with her family made it extra fun and special. This was our last time doing this hike before Janay started her new anchoring position in Maryland.

After that, we went out for Janay's birthday dinner at Mooney's Bar and Grill, which had the best mac n' cheese and chicken wings in town. Fortunately for me, her parents paid for everyone. Once again, I was grateful to have incredible people look after me during this hardship.

While we were having dinner, I received an email from the NJ Unemployment office. Early in the morning before church, I created my account to apply for unemployment and I received the confirmation email stating that I was good to go. I would receive over $700 a week, after-tax, and that was a huge blessing. My confidence grew as I thought about the money coming my way. I was also excited about tithing again. I had to catch up on what I could've tithed from the last job and yet whatever I could tithe during this time was a blessing. Now that I had money coming in, I had to invest every dollar purposefully in finding employment.

CHAPTER **15**

The Accidental Invite- October 4, 2019

As usual, I was spending a chunk of my unemployment days looking for open positions in Keller Williams and other real estate companies in the NYC Metro area. I applied to every position possible, outside of the sales agent. I drove to Hoboken for an interview where I was told I was overqualified. I drove to another interview where I took the MCA accounting test for the second time and wasn't invited back. I had phone interviews with what appeared to be sketchy companies in NYC. I was doing what it took to get back on my feet. Then, I got the call. It was a number from Washington, DC and I wasn't sure who it was. I answered the phone, and it was Rhonda, a KW broker. She called because I had applied for a position as an Inside Sales Agent (ISA) at her Keller Williams office and she wanted to meet me for an interview. In my mind, I had no idea what she was talking about. I didn't remember applying, let alone for a position in DC. Then I remembered that I may have come across it because I started to apply to jobs closer to Janay since she had moved to Maryland. Washington DC seemed reasonable, so why not? I agreed to meet with Rhonda the following week. When the day came, I headed out early to make the three-and-a-half-hour trip. However, I was having car issues and I emailed Rhonda telling her I was unable to make the trip. She told me to follow up with her when things were ok.

The truth is... my car didn't have issues. I punked out of the opportunity because I didn't want to make the drive. I had a limiting belief that if I wasn't getting hired back home, what difference would it be in DC? I also had responsibilities to my church, and I needed to be home.

A few days later, I got a call from DC. It was Rhonda again. I picked up the phone and we caught up. I apologized for not following up after my "incident" with the car. She forgave me and asked if I was still interested in the ISA position. With the feeling of desperation tugging at me, I told her yes and scheduled another interview with her for the following week. After I hung up, I realized something: I had to attend this time. I couldn't back out now. Also, this had to be a sign. Someone from Washington DC decided to follow up with an applicant from New Jersey and took the time to find out why. I told Rhonda I was looking to move closer to my fiancé and I wanted to join the

KW team somehow. Geographically, Washington DC was a safe bet. Even with that being the truth, it was a risky move and I didn't think ahead if I was offered a position (where would I live, how much would I have to make to survive, etc.). I didn't worry about all that at the time. All I knew was that I had an opportunity that aligned with what I was looking for and all I had to do was say, *yes now and figure it out later.*

CHAPTER 16

It's a Small World After All- October 9, 2019

It was 3:30 on a Wednesday morning and I was suited up for my interview. I said bye to my mom and brother, and I headed to the car. I plugged in my Bluetooth for music, cracked open a can of Celcius, my favorite healthy energy drink, and I hit the road. I was excited to drive to Washington DC as it has been a while since my last visit. During my senior year of college, George Washington University held a regional conference for an organization I was President of; Residence Hall Association (RHA). During that conference, my advisor, John, and I held leadership sessions and I was held up in board meetings for most of the weekend. I had my fun though. I discovered crepes for the first time that weekend, too. During this time, I would be driving to DC on my second unemployment check and I had to make every dollar worth it.

I entered DC around 10:00 AM and was relieved that the ride was nearly over. As expected, I hit morning traffic, and yet it wasn't bad enough to make me go crazy. Even then, I saw that as an opportunity to just jam out to some music and find the fun in it. Since the interview with Rhonda was at 1:00 PM, I decided to find parking down the street from her office and walk around and stretch from the trip.

Around noon, I went back to my car and drove closer to Rhonda's office to prepare for the interview. I found street parking a block away and stayed in my car until 12:40 PM. As usual, I did my final review of the position, the company, and read my affirmations. I was ready! I got out of my car, paid $2 for street parking and I headed off to the office. When I arrived, I entered an underground office that was decorated very well. I walked toward the middle of the office looking for Rhonda, only to find the training room full of agents in the middle of a session. I walked back toward the entrance and I saw a staff member and asked about Rhonda. They told me she was out of the office and she would be headed back shortly. So, I waited for Rhonda, standing awkwardly in the foyer. Then, a familiar face walked into the office; it was Jayson. Jayson and I were in the same mastermind and we met in-person for the first time back in April during an Neuro-Linguistic Programming (NLP) training. During that week, we got to train on NLP basics, and he was there with his KW team from Maryland. We even partnered up on an exercise. Then, on the last night of training, we hung out and I got to know him better. He told me his success story on how he started in real estate after college and how he worked his way in becoming a Team Leader (CEO in KW talk) of his current team. I realized I was hanging out with a million-dollar producer and it was an incredible opportunity to learn from one of the best.

It was a small world that Jayson and Rhonda were co-workers, and I was happy to see him. Before my interview, we sat in his office to catch up on what's been going on and I told him what I was looking for while I was in town. Then, I asked him about his new role for the region and he was still getting adjusted and yet he was loving it. During our quick chat, I couldn't shake the fact that I met this gentleman a few months back, and even though we kept in contact since, I would've never thought I had the possibility of working within the same field as him. As 1:00 PM approached, we ended our chat as Jayson had to get to an appointment himself. We shook hands and he told me to keep him posted on my visit. As he left through the doors, in came Rhonda and it was showtime!

CHAPTER 17

Maxing Out Potential-
October 9, 2019

After greeting Rhonda, she took me to the upstairs office, where the real main entrance was and sat me in one of the conference rooms. She was very personable, and she was a delight. We talked about my story and how I ended up in DC and what my goals were. We connected through my experience in ROTC the most. I told her I was medically disqualified from the program because of my history of heart problems, despite the strong evidence of my passing PT scores and leadership. She shared a similar experience when she was in ROTC in her college days and we both agreed on how the program helped us be stronger and more disciplined in life.

Then we talked about the ISA position. In its simplest form, an ISA would cold call leads the team generated and set appointments with said leads for agents. It was also a commission-only position. I emphasized to her that I was looking for a salaried position yet I was only willing to take commission-only if I really needed to. When asked about my sales experience, I shared that I had done a marketing internship as a door-to-door salesman in summer 2015 and developed "rhino skin" from hearing "no" for the most part. That was when I learned that every *no* was closer to a *yes*. I also shared that I did cold calls in my internship phase of being a financial advisor after I graduated from college, so I wasn't afraid of handling the phone. Rhonda tested that theory, and we role-played setting an buyer consultation. Using what I knew from my previous experience in sales and my recent experience in calling For Sale By Owners (FSBOs) for my real estate investment business, I was able to set the appointment...just barely. She got me with some "rebuttals", and it was clear that I had given into the demands of a potential client, having them set the tone for the next steps instead of me doing that.

After the first role-play, she gave me feedback on how to improve my call skills. Then, we role-played again, and I took her feedback and got better. This time, I set the appointment with "Kylie Jenner". She was impressed with the result.

After a few more minutes of feedback, Rhonda asked, "How long are you in town for?"

"I'll be here for the rest of the week," I said.

She then excused herself to make some calls. I waited patiently taking in what just occurred and felt pretty good about the interview. A few minutes later, Rhonda came back and told me what was next.

"Asher, I set an interview for you with Mr. Greene at our other office for tomorrow morning. He's looking for an operations manager for his team. Would you be able to make that?"

"Yes," I said.

She told Mr. Greene of my potential and catered to the need of finding a salary-based, position within the company, even though I had the sales skills she needed. I thanked her profusely and she said she'd be in touch and to keep her updated on the interview.

As I drove back to my hotel, I received a call from Rhonda. She told me that she set up another interview with another top agent named Steve for Friday afternoon. He was hiring for a marketing/operations position as well. Rhonda was the MVP of the week! I thanked her again and was super hyped as I approached the hotel. **WHAT...A...DAY!**

As I settled into my hotel room, I couldn't be more grateful for the success of the day. I went after an opportunity and it had blossomed into multiple opportunities. What did I do to deserve this? Then I remember my foundational scripture from the Bible, Matthew 7:7 KJV.

"Ask, and it shall be given you; seek, and ye shall find; knock, and it shall be opened unto you."

I've been knocking on many doors throughout the year and God has opened the right doors at the right time. Hallelujah!

CHAPTER **18**

The Hot Seat- October 10, 2019

It was 5:30 AM and I was ready to conquer the day. I took a shower, got dressed up, and headed down to the hotel lobby to grab some breakfast. I had more than enough time to enjoy it and look over the company details for my interview with Mr. Greene. I felt really good and I was excited to meet the owner and share what I could do for his company. After breakfast, I went to my car and drove to the office, which was about 30 minutes away. I got to the vicinity of the office nearly 40 minutes early and found free street parking a few blocks away. All I had to do was wait. I studied the company website and my interview questions some more and listened to some music.

Twenty minutes before the interview, I decided to walk to the office and arrive early. My rule for interviews is to show up at least 15 minutes early. **You either go early and be on time, show up on time and be**

late, or show up late and be forgotten. I prefer to be remembered.

When I got to the door, I was at my 15-minute mark and no one was answering. The door was locked, and I wasn't sure if I'd showed up a little too early or if I was even at the right place. Eventually, a secretary let me in as she arrived on the scene and seated me at a conference table.

After a few minutes, a gentleman with a three-piece suit walked in and greeted me kindly.

"Good morning, Asher. I'm Joel Greene. A pleasure to meet you".

"Likewise, sir," I replied.

Mr. Greene then moved our interview into a larger conference room with a TV and we sat down and talked. A few minutes into the interview, I started to get rattled and worried. When he was going through my resume, he was impressed with my experience, and yet one thing stuck out at him the most: my duration at the jobs. Just like my interview with Deeon, he wondered why I was switching from place to place in a short amount of time. I knew this was going to be an issue and I was ready to answer them truthfully and honestly. I told him my last job just let me go without explanation- which is true.

He then asked, "If I were to call your last supervisor, would he give a strong recommendation about you?"

I replied, "I think he would--"

"You think?" Mr. Greene interjected strongly.

"No. **I know** they will say that I worked hard and got things done for the team there".

He then took down his notes and we continued. He then asked about my experience in real estate investing and how many deals I have closed. At that point, I only did one buy and hold deal in the Poconos and I kicked out the tenants after six months because they stopped paying rent. It was clear that I didn't have enough experience in real estate. Mr. Greene was kind enough to share an overview about his company and what his plans were for the following year. The position I was interviewing for was meant for someone that understood the fundamentals of residential and commercial real estate, and he needed someone that can "hit the ground running."

I pleaded, "Mr. Greene, I know that my experience in real estate is scarce, but I am ready to take on anything and I'm passionate about learning this business so I can help the company succeed."

This sounded like a generic answer given at interviews... and it was. At that point, I didn't know how to sell myself to the level where he would feel confident with me in that position. I knew I wasn't going to get the job.

Finally, the grilling was over. Mr. Greene told me he'll follow up with my previous employer and will call me back for the next steps by next Friday. We shook hands and I headed back to the car. For the first time in a long time, I felt defeated coming out of an interview. The fact that I was considered for that type of job was a blessing and yet I knew I wouldn't be able to deliver at a high-level. When I got to my car, I just sat there for a few minutes and decided to head back to the hotel for the remainder of the day... until I got the text that changed everything.

CHAPTER 19

Meeting The McMasters-
October 10, 2019

As I was ready to buckle up and drive back to the hotel, I got a text from Jayson.

Jayson: GM bro. What's on your schedule today?

Asher: Good morning man. Just finished meeting with Mr. Greene. You? I may head back to the hotel.

Jayson: Ok. I'm going to link you with Robert so y'all can get together. Can you make 11AM?

Asher: Ok. Thanks man. I'm still at Mr. Greene's office so I'll stick around up here. And yes. Where at?

He gave me the office address, which was in Northeast DC.

Asher: Thanks. I'll head over there right now. Dude, I think I messed up that interview.

Jayson: Just knock out this one at 11AM. Robert is who you are meeting with.

I had an hour to get to the next interview and I was only 20 minutes away. I don't like to play around with extra time if I have it, so I just drove to the vicinity of the office and found metered parking a block away. I sat in my car until 20 minutes before going into the office. I didn't look up what the company was about or even googled who Robert was. All I knew was that I had another opportunity to share my passion to contribute growth to someone who may need it.

After I said my affirmations, I put money in the meter and walked to the office. The office was a huge grey, warehouse-like building that had a big M on top and had a name spelled "Menkiti Group". I walked inside and met the receptionist, Katie. I told her I had an 11 AM meeting with Robert and she told me to take a seat in the lobby while she went to get him. A few minutes later, I was met with a tall dude with glasses and a vibe so chill, it was very welcoming.

"What's up, man? My name is Robert."

"I'm Asher. A pleasure to meet you, sir."

When we got to Robert's office, he introduced me to a lovely woman named Ashley, his wife, and business partner. We shook hands and I took a seat on their very comfortable sofa and we got down to business.

From the start of the meeting, The McMasters assured me to not be nervous and to just let loose. We were just having a conversation and getting to know each other. That was comforting to hear as I was still getting rid of the jitters from the last interview with Mr. Greene. The McMasters asked what I was doing in DC from New Jersey and I explained the whole backstory from my last position to getting my license, to this point of my journey. They shared their story on how they got started in real estate and it was an incredible story. Robert served in the Air Force for over 10 years, then left to be with Ashley to build a family together. He worked for the government for a few years working in presidential transportation amongst other things and decided to leave his government job after gaining traction in doing real estate part-time. He earned *Rookie of the Year* in 2014 and hasn't looked back since. Now, he is the Managing Director of the sales team.

Ashley has a background in accounting, so when I shared my experience in finance and a desire to switch to real estate, she completely understood where I was coming from. She got Robert to get his real estate license to supplement their income and then got her real estate license for all the DMV as well and made an impressive amount of sales herself. She is currently the Director of Sales for the team. The McMasters were a power couple. They were the role models I had been looking for. When I saw their picture on the Washingtonian plaque for being "Team of the Year". I got this spark inside me that confirmed I was with the right people.

We spoke more in detail about who they needed for their growing team. I had met them while a merger was in process between them and The Menkitis. The Menkitis are just as incredible. They are another power couple from the DC area and have made a significant impact on the DC community over the last decade. What I didn't realize until later was that I was in the building of the founder and CEO of the Menkiti Group as well as the Operating Principal of Keller Williams Capital Properties, the brokerage for the region. I was at the heart of the whole region with the top 1% of agents recognized by Gary Keller himself. What did I do to deserve this?

The position the McMasters were creating was the Operations Coordinator position that would ensure quality control of current processes of the team as well as creating new ones that would benefit the team and putting Standard Operating Procedures (SOPs) together. They were also looking for an Inside Sales Agent that would make calls daily to leads that inquired about their services from internet sources. They also asked about my DISC assessment and KPA. The DISC assessment is another personality test that determines how one functions in a work environment, similar to the KPA I did with Steve, and Deeon.

Because of my DISC, KPA, resume, and real estate license, Robert and Ashley decided to push me to the next step of the interview process and scheduled a Career Visioning (CV) interview for the following Tuesday. I held my excitement until I left the building and yet I showed my gratitude to the leaders upon leaving. I even helped them out by booking them a hotel room with the friends and family discount rate at the Gaylord Convention Center for Columbus Weekend. That helps with my candidacy, right?

When I left the office, I walked with new energy and hope compared to the last interview. "What just happened," I thought in amazement. I still couldn't believe it. Even though it was still early in the interview process, I knew that this was a step forward toward my destiny and I was very confident in the rest of the process. I texted Jayson on what happened, and he shared his excitement. He told me to keep him updated throughout the process.

I got back to my car and screamed in excitement and joy. I'm on my way. **I have God by my side, and I trust in Him.** This was the beginning of something big and I would continue to walk by faith. For the rest of the week, I continued to work on myself at the hotel and prepared for the last interview of the week with Steve for the marketing position. Even though the interview went well, nothing came out of it. I was able to spend quality time with Janay for the remainder of the weekend when she was off work. I drove back home with a new sense of confidence, and faith and I couldn't wait to build upon my vision to be a real estate professional.

CHAPTER **20**

Digging Into the Vision-
October 15, 2019

It was a Tuesday morning, and I was ready for the second part of my interview, Career Visioning (CV). The CV was a lengthy process that was different from any other interview process I'd ever been through. It goes into detail of what your goals are in your career and life. Thankfully, my KPA had a template of how the CV would go and what questions would be asked. I had taken time the night before to prepare for this. Ashley ran the CV process through Zoom and it was a rocky start. The first part of the CV goes through my resume. At first, I was following the resume as-is and sharing details about my club organizations that add on the resume Then I started to explain my responsibilities from my previous job in greater detail. While I was explaining my last position, Ashley stopped me for a second.

"Asher. I can see what you did in your last position. The point of this exercise is to know what led to these events. What happened in between, who was there, etc. I want to know who Asher, the person is, not Asher the financial analyst."

I was stumped on this for a second. I was so used to explaining what was on the paper and now I had to explain what was happening within me during these times. This is what makes the CV unique and from that point on, I honored the integrity of it. One of the other questions she asked was to share a time where I did something for someone, even when it put myself at risk (or something like).

I told her about the time I decided to move out of my mom's house in early 2018 and live in an apartment closer to my previous job. The only way I was able to afford rent was by taking out a loan and using some savings. I kept that money in another account and used it as needed. Fast forward to early summer, I was visiting my mom on a weekend. It was about 7:00 PM and we were just catching up. As the night went on, she ended up going upstairs to her room and I hung out at the computer in the living room, working on real estate deals. Suddenly, the lights went out in the entire house. I went to the basement to check on the breakers and there wasn't a problem with that. We checked the other light switches, and nothing was coming on. Eventually, we realized that the electric company cut the power out because the bill was past due. As I was headed back upstairs to bring a candle for the basement bedroom,

I remember my mom sitting down at the top of the steps and she started to tear up. I haven't seen her cry like this before. It was heart-breaking and you could really feel a sense of hopelessness. I sat next to her to comfort her and told her everything was going to be alright. She went through Hell and high water to bring my brother and me out of Jersey City and invested all that she could to give us a great life.

After I consoled her, I called the electric company and negotiated a payment arrangement for her. I was able to set an arrangement, with the first payment being made that night and the second payment being made the next week. The reason why they cut off the services was due to insufficient funds in her account. After hearing this, I decided to pay for the first half of the arrangement to give my mom some breathing room until her next payday. I had to pay my rent in a few days and yet, I had enough cushion from picking up extra hours from work. Because the internet was down, I had to drive to my friend's house down the street and pay the bill online on my phone. I paid the first payment, and the lights were back on an hour later. The next week, I paid for the second half as well as the upcoming month's bill, so my mother could have more room for taking care of other things. I used the loan money to cover that. I was happy I was able to help her, even though I risked being late for rent or not having enough at all. That didn't matter to me. It was making sure that family was taken care of, which pushed me to work hard for all these years.

After that, Ashley continued the interview and then we had to stop due to time constraints. We scheduled the second part of the CV for the following Tuesday and I crushed it.

The CV went deeper than I expected and it was great to know that my potential employers were interested in what made me who I am; what made me tick as a person and how I could leverage that to accomplish the goals and dreams I set for myself. I even learned a lot about myself during the CV. I was setting goals that felt so out of my reach, I thought I was crazy. Nevertheless, I kept pushing and made way for what's possible. After the completion of the CV, I was invited back to DC to do a final group interview with the team, which would determine the rest of my life.

CHAPTER 21

The Room Reservation-
October 18, 2020

Every year since I graduated college, I plan a visit to Penn State for one of the best events of the college football season: The White Out Game. It's a special home game that's reserved for Penn State's top rivals, Ohio State and the University of Michigan. The game was an event that brought students, faculty, and alumni together for one weekend and witnessed the decimation of the opponent in "white-out conditions". It's called a whiteout because fans wear white and when brought together under the lights, it's a beautiful sight to see for Penn State fans, and it's a daunting environment for the visiting team. This year, we hosted Michigan, and leading up to the game, Penn State was slated to win.

This White Out was special because my great friend, Malcolm, was attending his first White Out game. He's visited University Park a few times before for other games and our Blue and White weekend and he's yet to experience why Penn State has the GREATEST STUDENT SECTION OF ALL TIME! We had planned to go since last year and I had booked our hotel room then. The closest room we could get was in Williamsport, Pennsylvania- which was 45 minutes away from the campus.

Even with everything going on with my interview in DC and living off unemployment, I had saved enough to cover gas, food, and the biggest expense- my half of the hotel room. We'd already bought the tickets two weeks prior.

On that Friday, Malcolm drove down to my house from Connecticut and I drove us to Pennsylvania. We got to Penn State a little later than planned and yet we still had time to grab food and hang out downtown.

Late that night, we got to the hotel, grabbed our things from the car, and headed to check-in. I gave the front desk clerk my card for incidentals, then worry struck.

"I'm sorry, Mr. Carr. The card is not going through due to insufficient funds."

In my head, I thought, "How is that possible? I just had enough money for the weekend! And why did she announce that as loud as possible? The disrespect!"

I checked my bank app and saw there was a payment that had been taken out for my phone bill. I wouldn't get my next unemployment check until that Tuesday. I knew I had to ask Malcolm for help and yet I was embarrassed to do so.

Sucking it up, I told Malcolm what happened, and I asked if he could cover the room for the weekend and I would pay him back by Tuesday. Even though the incidental was refundable, I gave myself some time to get the money for my half.

He thought about it for a moment, and then he said, "Bet!"

He covered the room for us, and relief dwelled over me. We got our room keys, got to our room, and settled in. I apologized to Malcolm profusely about the check-in mishap and how grateful I was for his help. Even with our strong friendship, I kept quiet about my unemployment situation all year and had always been insecure about asking for help.

I thought, "What if he didn't have enough himself? What would've been the plan then?"

I'm just grateful that God provided what we needed in that situation and that He placed a great friend in my life that didn't judge me for a small oversight.

CHAPTER 22

Tapping Into the Family Network- October 19, 2019

It's game day! Malcolm and I woke up with joy and got ourselves together for the day's festivities. While I was getting ready, Malcolm checked his GoPro equipment to capture the spectacular moments to come. He's a photographer and videographer part-time and has a keen sense of vision for his art. He planned to document the whole weekend for his next project. Once he was set, we grabbed breakfast and headed off to campus.

There was so much going on leading up to the big game. ESPN was on campus for the weekly College GameDay segment and there was a flood of white shirts at the student center lawn, where students and fans showed off their school spirit on national television. Malcolm captured great B-Roll for his video and even got a picture with the Orange College GameDay bus. Then we walked around campus for more video and pictures, before making our way down to College

Avenue, where all the hustle and bustle was and ended up at our favorite clothing store, Lion and Cub, to grab a new hoodie for the game. After more B-Roll of the downtown, we met up with several of my close friends for tailgating.

The first tailgate was with my former work-study supervisor, Donna. During my time at Penn State, I worked in the Office of Student Life (OSL) with Donna, the Finance Chair, Dani, the Director of OSL, Ginny, the Administrative Support Associate of OSL, and Nikki and Jessie, the Associate Directors of OSL. There were also graduate assistants that rotated out of the office as well. The last graduate assistant I worked with was Noah. This team was responsible for many of the student events that took place throughout the school year. From dances to concerts to bingo nights, it was never a dull moment working in OSL and working with student leadership. I learned so much about leadership and making life decisions from each of the ladies, and Noah, over the years, and I couldn't be more grateful for the family-oriented environment they fostered in college. Student Life was the primary reason for my growth as a leader and person. Donna, in particular, became my "mother away from home" and that connection holds strong to this day.

Malcolm and I got to Donna's tailgate and settled in. Catching up with Donna, we talked about what has been going on with the job situation. Donna always had incredible insight on what to do when making a career move.

From the beginning, Donna knew how passionate I was in helping others and being a leader in my field. It was just a matter of where and when, and that time would soon come. I told her about my interview in DC and she was excited for me and told me to keep pushing through. I was on my way. This is why I visit my Alma Mater when I can. It wasn't the degree, accolades, or football games that made my college experience memorable. It was the people that shaped me into a better person. The people who saw something in me that I didn't see in myself. The people that invested the time and energy to ensure my success beyond college and making sure I stayed the course. This is beyond networking. This is a family. I am grateful for Donna and the other leaders I've worked with in my college days and continue to work with today. When I'm ready to give back to my university, it wouldn't just be in scholarships. It would be in sharing compassion and the love of winning and learning in life and seeing the next person change the world in their way.

For the remainder of the tailgate, I presented a "degree" in Penn State Football to Malcolm as a gift for his incredible friendship and huge support and love for the team. In some cases, he is a bigger fan than I am. With some help from Donna, I was able to find the best novelty gift to make the weekend memorable for him. After spending time with Donna, Malcolm and I headed to another tailgate where I met with my health and wellness coaches, and great friends, Craig and Bethany, before getting dinner. Craig and Bethany were Orientation Leaders with me in college and Bethany was my teammate in my last season of cheerleading in 2015. She also helped me accomplish my backflip that season. They graduated in 2017 and we stayed in touch through our common interest in finding passion in our craft. They also helped me find my groove in the gym and I lost 20 pounds on the fitness program I was testing for them during my job hunt. It was much needed and I felt healthier, compared to when I was in finance. White Out weekend was a great time to catch up with friends and family who also loved Penn State football. At the moment, everything in life felt great.

CHAPTER 23

For the Love of Football and Family- October 19, 2019

Before we headed to the stadium, Malcolm and I got dinner at our favorite Chinese spot downtown. I received a call headed downstairs to the restaurant and it was urgent, so I gave Malcolm some cash to order our food. I answered the phone, and it was my Tita (Aunt in Tagalog) Connie. Tita Connie worked at the Marriott with my mother and she has been fantastic to our family for as long as I can remember. I called her the night before for some help to get through the weekend. I explained what happened at check-in and without question, she offered to send me money. She had her daughter Venmo me $300 to cover the hotel plus some for the rest of the weekend.

I told her I would pay her back that same week and she said, "Don't worry about it. No rush. Pay when you can."

After the call, I met up with Malcolm for dinner and then we headed toward the stadium to grab our seats. For the remainder of the night, we were in awe of the school spirit and blinding white shirts around the stadium. We had a great time and Penn State beat Michigan... just barely (Google *Penn State vs. Michigan 2019* and see how stressful the second half was for us). Malcolm's first White Out game was a success! Another memorable time in Happy Valley was in the books.

One thing I learned during White Out weekend was the amount of love that was in my life. Outside of my immediate family, It was love that was recognized and yet, underutilized. Growing up, I've had incredible family and friends who have gone above and beyond to help me succeed (I.e. OSL) and I would feel weird receiving such help because it would come as unconventional help. I had a limiting belief that my cry for help makes people step out of THEIR comfort zone. It's ME that is stepping out of my comfort zone and reaching out for something I needed assistance with, especially with money. Money can make things weird and I tread carefully when asking for other people's money. However, in asking for help from Donna, I was able to make the right decisions in my career path and keep the faith. Also, in asking for help from Tita Connie, I made sure I was able to go to someone I could trust and knew that I could payback. Thanks to her, I was able to pay Malcolm back the next day and a few days after that, I was able to pay her back in full after re-budgeting.

You may be thinking it was stupid of me to go to a football game I could barely afford. The truth of the matter is that it wasn't that *I couldn't afford to go*; it was figuring out *how I could afford it, and how I could be flexible in making it happen.* Even when things seem bad, nothing can ever stop me from experiencing the things that make me who I am and spending time with those I love.

CHAPTER 24

The Final Round-
November 14, 2019

A few weeks had gone by since the CV interview with Ashley. At this point, we're nearing Thanksgiving and I was starting to get worried. My limiting beliefs started to kick in. *What if this is the same outcome as my interview in the Bronx? Are the regional leaders questioning the sustainability of commuting to the office? Do they know that I was willing to move if offered the job? What's taking so long?*

I was hesitant in reaching out because I felt that doing so would make me look too pushy. Again, the limiting beliefs I had were ridiculous. **I must act now!**

I texted Ashley for an update on the group interview date. She replied and said they had been slammed with business and wanted to get the team together on a day they would be in the office at one time. That made sense. She told me she would follow up with an exact date by the end of the week. Sure enough, Ashley texted me a few days later and set a date for Monday, November 18th at noon. Let's go!

I was excited and nervous. This was the interview that could change the course of my life. I had to sell myself to some of the top producers on the sales team and operations team. I'd been in this situation before though. The key to these interviews is being myself. It's all about showing who I am and sharing how I can contribute to the team. Even though the interview rooms tend to feel cold with the expectation of the interviewers grilling you with pressing questions, I felt pretty good about it and couldn't wait to take another three and a half-hour drive back to the nation's capital. The night before, I decided to drive to a hotel in Bethesda to get the trip out the way, so I could focus on preparation for the group interview.

And yes, I had more than enough money this time at check-in.

CHAPTER 25

Opportunity With a Side of Gravy- November 18, 2019

I woke up the next morning around 7:30 to start my morning routine: affirmations, work out, affirmations again, and final studies on the team and their latest projects. Then, I ate breakfast and eventually checked-out to drive to the interview. I was surprised at how easy the drive was on a Monday morning. One thing I learned during my last visit was that DC traffic was FAR WORSE than NYC. I didn't think it was possible.

I arrived at the office in 20 minutes and found near-by street parking. I still had 20 minutes until the interview, so I read my affirmations one more time, prayed, and marched out of my car to the interview. In the words of Kevin Hart, "IT'S ABOUT TO GO DOWN!"

I arrived at the front desk, where I met Katie again and told her I was here for a group interview with Ashley. She sent the message through, came back, and told me to wait in the lobby as they were finishing a sales meeting. I sat down and noticed some activity going on a few feet away from me. In the office kitchen, there was a long table with trays of food and bottles of drinks. There was a dessert table, too. Then, I remembered that Ashley had mentioned something about a Friendsgiving lunch at the office during my interview. That's cool. I don't recall attending a Friendsgiving before.

I waited 15 minutes for Ashley. Then nearly another 15 minutes after that. It was 12:15 already. That sales meeting was taking a while. What were they talking about in there? I did hear laughing at some point, too. What was that about? Eventually, the conference room opened, and out came Ashley. She called me over and welcomed me back. She told me that the team was ready to meet with me and walked me toward the head of the conference room table where I sat with the members of the team. Ashley introduced me to the interviewers and then left to help prepare for the Friendsgiving event.

I was seated at the table with high-profile agents and staff. There were John and Marie Claire, who were buyer specialists, Virginia, a listing specialist, and Shulisa the Marketing Coordinator for the team, and the only operations person at that point.

I introduced myself and opened with this statement, "I am here to interview for the Operations Coordinator position. I am a licensed realtor in New Jersey, and I received my license so I can have a better understanding of how agents operate, so I can serve you better. I am excited to join a team and contribute in any way I can through this position".

I don't remember much yet I do remember laughs,and how my time in ROTC could serve the team. We even talked about utilizing faith. Also, the room wasn't as cold as expected and the interview was filled with warmth, which made me feel confident. I didn't even get grilled as expected either. After about 15 minutes, the interview was over, and I shared my gratitude with the group. I was ready to head home.

As I was headed toward the front door, Ashley met with me at the front desk and asked how the interview went. I told her it went very well and expressed my gratitude for the opportunity again. She then invited me to stay for lunch and join the Friendsgiving event.

"Are you sure?" I asked.

"Yeah, of course. Let me take your binder and you can join the rest of the group."

I didn't know how I felt about this. *Was this part of the interview process?*

Leaning on my ability to adjust to my environment, and giving into my starving stomach, I embraced the invite and got in line for food. Someone welcomed me to the table and told me to get a plate and help myself.

I got in line behind John, the agent that had interviewed me earlier.

"Food looks good man," he said.

"Yeah. A lot of options." I replied.

I then asked my golden question when networking, "So, what's your story?"

He then shared how his father was in the Army and he'd grown up moving around a lot. He then got into real estate after working in the non-profit sector, and saw what it could provide for his family and had been with the team since 2016. John had this cool vibe about him, and he seemed to be enjoying his life as a realtor. As he went to sit down to eat, he wished me luck on the rest of the interview.

After filling up my plate, I went over to the training room across the hall, where other staff members and agents were eating. I sat down, blessed my food, and started eating, with the continuing thought of *what are they testing me with?* Then I decided to stop overthinking and just enjoy the food.

A guy sat next to me and introduced himself as Lawrence.

I asked him the golden question as well, "So, what's your story?"

Lawrence was originally from Morristown, NJ, and had a background in finance. He was an account manager for the Menkiti Group and had been with the team for a few months. We shared a few laughs about living in New Jersey amongst other things. As I continued to eat my lunch, another person sat next to me with his plate.

High off the energy from talking with Lawrence, I introduced myself right away. "Hi. I'm Asher. How are you?"

"Hi Asher. I'm Bo. Nice to finally meet you."

I couldn't believe it. I was having Friendsgiving lunch with the Founder and CEO of the Menkiti Group. I thought to myself, "This is definitely a test."

Bo recently completed a phase on a massive project in DC and I congratulated him on that. Then I asked him about some projects going on in Worcester, MA, and how those started. He told me that's where he was originally from and explained the backstory on that. Of course, I knew that. He then asked me about my goals, and I shared how I wanted to build out a great operations team, help sell some real estate, then look into real estate development in the long-term. I told him that my family had real estate in the Philippines and I wanted to learn how to take advantage of that when the time comes.

After a few minutes of conversation, he had to go to a meeting.

"It was nice speaking with you Asher. I wish you the best in your interview."

Lawrence also had to get back to work.

"It was a pleasure meeting you, Asher. I hope to work with you soon."

For the remainder of the lunch, I stayed until the end and was ready to head out. I also remembered that I had a two-hour parking limit, and I was well over that. Ashley told me they would speak with the team about the group interview and get back to me ASAP on a final decision. She also mentioned that she spoke with Deeon from New York and emphasized how much praise he gave me. That helped boost my sense of confidence in joining the team.

After saying our goodbyes, I grabbed my binder and lightly jogged to my car. Fortunately, there wasn't a parking ticket there. I got inside the car and sat there with a sense of gratitude, relief, and hope.

"It was a good day," I thought, and it was only 2:00 PM. It was hands down my favorite group interview I'd ever done.

From that moment on, I was speaking affirmation into existence saying, "I am a team member for Keller Williams, and I will serve this team at a high level."

There wasn't an ounce of doubt or worry within me anymore. I knew God was setting up the finale.

CHAPTER 26

Playing Agent-
November 20, 2019

Even though I wasn't given an official offer to join the team yet, I took a leap of faith and started my search for housing. Janay had already connected me with Facebook groups focused on potential renters asking for openings within DC or Maryland. Fortunately, I was able to connect with a landlord that held several rental properties in Silver Spring, Bethesda, and Gaithersburg. His name was AJ, and we connected right away. AJ was a Penn State Alum, and he was managing properties from State College. He was also the founder of Broken Ear Buttons, which were custom-made buttons that poked fun at opposing teams during football season. During our conversation, I shared that I was working in DC with a real estate team and he asked if I could help market two of his rentals in Silver Spring. He offered to pay me a flat fee for my work plus a free set of the 2019 Broken Ear Buttons. On top of that, he would help me get housing at one of his other rentals. At that point, any opportunity to make money, within reason, was an opportunity I was willing to take. Plus, those buttons were hilarious.

At first, he sent me his current Craigslist ads for the rentals. The descriptions were very long, and the post had to be redone ASAP. I optimized the ads the same way I optimized my rentals back home: Short, sweet and to the point. From my experience, all people need to know is price, what's included, availability, and pictures. I showed the new ads to DJ and he approved. A few hours later, I started getting traction and my phone was blowing up with inquiries. I would vet the leads to make sure they were legit and then forward them to AJ for the next steps. He would then schedule times with his property manager/tenant at the locations for walkthroughs. Even though we were getting a substantial amount of interest, it took a while until someone signed the paperwork and gave a deposit for one of the rentals. The second rental was filled by a family friend of AJs.

AJ messaged me after both rentals were fulfilled to thank me for my contribution and said he would pay me once the first month's rent was due. He even offered a room at a discount for me to stay at in his Bethesda rental. My search for housing was over. Even though I didn't make a killing, I was happy to assist. I related to the struggle of finding quality tenants, especially if Craigslist was being utilized. I used the same tactics for him as I used when I was promoting rental space for my mom back at home. She decided to rent out the basement after getting it renovated while I was in high school. Surprisingly, Craigslist brought well-qualified tenants to our house and over the years, my mother had little to no issues with tenants, except for one guy and his crazy girlfriend.

During the time of helping AJ, I gained experience on marketing a rental and qualifying potential tenants. Unofficially, AJ was my client, and I took time every day to check up the rental posts, respond to inquiries, market on Facebook, and use a third-party leasing site to give the rentals more exposure. I was tapping into my inner agent and, for the most part, I was confident in what I was doing. Even though the money wasn't a lot, I was given an opportunity to help someone and that is my passion. Real estate can truly transform lives at every level. No client is too big or too small and everyone deserves to have a roof over their head.

CHAPTER 27

A Filipino Thanksgiving- November 28, 2019

Though this wasn't how I expected the year to go, nothing beats the spirit of Thanksgiving. Growing up, my mom would host a big family Thanksgiving party for our relatives, and everyone would bring a dish to share for dinner. Growing up in a Filipino household, I had the most authentic Filipino food you could get. From appetizers to main entrees like pancit, lumpia rolls, and lechon, to desserts such as turon, and halo-halo, my childhood was wrapped up in the culinary arts of Southeast Asian cuisine. I have my love for American food, and yet nothing is as great as moms cooking. Over the years, my mom stopped hosting the parties and we just kept Thanksgiving dinners small. This year, I wanted to make Thanksgiving special and give my mom a break from cooking. I would cook the dinner so she wouldn't have to rush back home from New York and get everything set up. Plus, I was low-key a decent chef...I said what I said.

Earlier in the week, I went to Sam's Club to pick up my menu for Thanksgiving dinner, plus additional groceries for the house. On Thanksgiving Day, it was a full day of family, friends, and food. I spent half the afternoon with Janay and her family at her cousins house around the corner. I did my best to not eat too much before I had to cook back home. Around 4:00 PM, I headed home to start prep work for my dinner, and it was Iron Chef time. The menu of the night was the following:

Garden Salad
Salmon with Honey Glazed Sauce
Steak marinated in Garlic
and Herb Butter Sauce
Baked Ziti
Mashed Potatoes made
from scratch
Sam's Club Pumpkin Pie
Vanilla Ice Cream

Turkey hadn't made the cut for a few years already. If anything, a holiday ham was the star of a Filipino Thanksgiving and yet that didn't make the menu this year either.

I was excited to serve dinner for the family, even if it was just my mom, brother and myself. Being able to do this amid the struggle meant that things were going to get better. As I shared before, family is part of the reason why I push myself to become successful in what I do. Being unemployed didn't hinder me from reaching greatness and God knows all things. This holiday, I was just happy to have a roof over my head and be around my loved ones. This was my gift to my mother and brother for supporting me during this tough time. Home is truly where the heart is, and I am grateful for my family.

CHAPTER 28

Standing at the Door of Opportunity- December 3, 2019

A week after the group interview, Ashley called me about the results of the interview. With sweaty palms from being anxious, I answered the phone and got to talking. Ashley told me that the team liked me a lot and they approved of me coming on board.

"Congratulations. You are now part of the team", she said.

It was a dream come true. I couldn't believe it and yet I knew this day would come. I gave thanks and she informed me that she would send the final paperwork within the week for review and signature.

Everything I had to do that led to that point was worth it. The amount of money spent on getting my license and driving to different interviews for KW. The amount of time spent on learning about KW and an industry I had yet to join. The decisions to not look back at what was and continuing to look forward in faith. It was all worth it. I was on my way in fulfilling my real estate career dreams and I thank God for what He's done for me.

Due to heavy traffic in business, my start date moved from December 2nd to December 9th. When I received my letter, I read through the official responsibilities of my newly created position, *Operations Support Specialist*. It was weird to read that because during the interview process, the title was *Operations Coordinator;* that had a better ring to it. Either way, I didn't get caught up with the title for very long. I learned early in the workforce that titles are only temporary. It's all about having the mentality of the position one desires.

There is a saying, "Dress up for the job you want, not for the one you have."

I continued to read through my package and got to the compensation section. During the interview, we didn't talk too much about compensation, and yet I did hint that I was making close to six-figures as an analyst when asked. When I saw what they offered me, my heart stopped, and I wasn't sure what to do next. My base salary was nearly *half* of what I made as an analyst. I wasn't expecting to make the same amount right off the back; maybe $10,000 to $20,000 less at most. At the time, the salary seemed like a slap to the face.

However, there was a commission part of the offer that would hold some promise: a *flat fee bonus for every appointment set and held*. I remembered that they needed an Inside Sales Agent as well. I would be playing two roles for the team, which I thought was pretty cool. Although, I was still uncertain how much that could bring me. My history in sales wasn't as great as it might have seemed during the interview. I had seen moderate success in setting appointments as a Financial Advisor and that's what I would think about when it came to sales.

To be frank, I wasn't 100 percent confident in my sales skills and I asked myself, "Was everything I had just gone through worth this much money?"

CHAPTER 29

Knowing My True Worth- December 5, 2019

I was getting ready to head to Staples in the morning and reluctantly send over the paperwork for the position. I didn't sign anything yet and I needed some insight on how to make the best out of this opportunity. I had come too far to back out. On my way to Staples, I called my long-time college friend, Atta. We go way back to my first year of college. He was a junior who was also an RA at the time, and we roomed together in Spruce Hall, the other residence hall with suite-style rooms. We connected through the business program we were both involved in at school and always stayed in contact. I even let him borrow my car during his senior year when he lived off-campus and he took very good care of it. He's originally from Brooklyn, so it was easy to hang out and catch up throughout the years. I consider him as one of my "friends for life", thanks to Penn State.

Atta was one of the few people I told about getting let go and with having a few years ahead of me in the business world, he was a relatable person to go to.

I explained the situation to him, and he asked me the tough questions such as, "Can you live off that much a month? Or less than that after taxes? How are you going to keep yourself fed after the bills are paid?"

He also shared how he was nervous, too, when he started his new position and yet he made it possible because he planned accordingly.

"Planned accordingly? How?" I asked.

Because of the commission structure in place, he was able to break down how much he needed to make in sales to pay off the bills and have a cushion for everything else. That was the best way in making sure he took home enough money for him and his family. With a base salary, it made working for commission easier and in a way, exciting. What I appreciated about Atta was how he always asked me how I felt about things. In a way, he saw something in me that I didn't. He suggested that push for an increase in salary by $10,000, given the current circumstances. If that didn't work, then I would have to sink or swim.

When I got to Staples, I looked at the papers again and read through them one more time. Then I closed my eyes and prayed on it. If God brought me down to Washington DC from New Jersey on unemployment money to fulfill my desire in real estate, there had to be a bigger reason than the money itself.

Proverbs 3:5-6-KJV says, "Trust in the Lord with all thine heart; and lean not unto thine own understanding. In all thy ways acknowledge him, and he shall direct thy paths."

Throughout the whole year, I had made plans to start my real estate career and join the Keller Williams family. I had the opportunity in my hands to solidify that and yet I wasn't sure because I didn't have faith in my skill set, and I was judging my future based on a salary. I had to remind myself of a few things:

1. A smaller salary is better than no salary at all.
2. I made a move to DC by faith and not by sight, and
3. The story isn't over, and my faith is being tested even more now.

After having my epiphany from God and taking in Atta's advice, I signed off on the papers and went into Staples to scan them for Ashley. It's official: I am the Operations Support Specialist for a Keller Williams team and I am going to make the best out of this position because I have God and my faith will be unwavered.

CHAPTER 30

Cheers to Real Estate Careers-December 7, 2019

The Saturday before my first day, I was invited to my first team event called "Cheers to Real Estate Careers." It was a networking event inviting those that were interested in becoming real estate professionals and the sales team displayed the talent and opportunities given within the team and the brokerage. I showed up an hour early to help set up and got to know Shulisa, the Marketing Coordinator, and Maya, the former Operations Coordinator. The highlight of the morning was making Mimosas and we learned how NOT to make them. People love champagne, though, right? They'll be just fine.

About 30 minutes before the event, the office space began filling up with attendees and everyone was grabbing food, drink, and taking a seat in the training room, where a panel of agents and brokerage members would be presenting. The first part of the event included agents from the sales team with different levels of experience. Each person talked about their experience on the team and the opportunities that helped them become successful including personalized coaching, dual-career growth, and a plethora of resources.

One speaker that stood out to me the most was Marie Claire. She had been an agent with the team for some time and shared something I wasn't expecting in a work environment, let alone at a professional networking event: the word of God. She referenced a book called "God is a Salesman" and connected how the work of Jesus is similar to the work done in real estate. She also shared how her faith pulled her through the tough challenges that real estate brought and how that impacts the client's faith in the agent. Through her faith, she was able to see success in her business and the blessings continued to flow.

It was incredible to hear someone share their faith in a room full of diversity and not be ashamed. I was taught that sharing one's religious belief was frowned upon in the workforce and could stir up controversy in the office. However, at that moment, It was another sign that I was in the right place. As Marie Claire shared her faith, there were head nods around the room, agreeing with her. I later found out that Marie Claire had a Pentecostal background and we connected through that. It was great to know that even at work, I would be around followers of Christ and have the freedom to talk about my faith without fear.

The second part of the panel included a talk from Robert and Jayson. Both shared a piece of how they got into real estate and gave wise advice on how to succeed. One powerful message they shared was about accountability and how coaching was a must in the business. Robert shared how investing time and money for coaching made an impact on his business and his life.

"An accountability partner that is a stranger is the most powerful thing you can have in this business. If there is someone doing something you want to do, get with them and then use them as an accountability partner because it's going to help excel you. You will be accountable to a stranger- trust and believe it."

Jayson expanded on the concept by sharing the three types of accountability:

1. **Finding a mentor: Connecting with someone that is ahead of the game and you can look up to.**
2. **Peer mentoring: Connecting with someone, or a tribe of people, on the same boat going toward the same direction.**
3. **Teaching someone who is behind you: Connecting with someone who is new to the business and teaching them how to succeed.**

Jayson emphasized, "The greatest form of mastery is having to teach it."

It was clear that real estate was not just an individual sport. It takes a team to succeed at a high level and I was grateful to have the opportunity to contribute to a team that was looking to accelerate in their production.

After Robert and Jayson closed off the event, many people stayed to network with the team. I stayed toward the very end, helping with the breakdown and cleaning the space.

On my way out, I said bye to Ashley, and she asked, "Are you still good for tomorrow night?"

I had no idea what she was talking about and then I remembered she gave me a ticket to the Washington Wizards Basketball game in the company suite.

"Yep. I'll be there. I'll see you then."

CHAPTER 31

Hanging Out with the All-Stars- December 8, 2019

It was 6:30 PM and I was headed out to catch the train to Capital One Arena. I was excited to go to my first NBA game and experience it in style. I got to the arena a little past 7:30 PM and made my way up to the suite level to meet with Ashley and Robert. When I got to the suite, I was greeted by the event staff and met a few people from the team's title company who had arrived early. Ashley and Robert didn't arrive yet. I put my coat on the rack and grabbed a seat in the skybox while I waited for the others to arrive. It was very awkward at first just sitting there and yet I realized what I was looking at. I had a bird's eye view of Capital One Arena and I was going to witness my first NBA game with my new colleagues before I even started work. This was incredible. That night, the Wizards were hosting the Los Angeles Clippers and that meant one thing: **KAWHII LEONARD WAS IN THE BUILDING!** He was crowned the MVP of the playoffs last season when he was with the Toronto Raptors. If anyone knew about basketball, they knew that Kawhi was a talented player with an interesting personality (Insert Kawhii laugh here).

A few minutes into the first quarter, more people showed up to the suite, including the McMasters and some of the sales team. A chef also entered and started bringing in large appetizers that consisted of chicken strips, wings, and nachos. Very diverse menu, if you ask me. I grabbed a plate of food and as I went back to my seat, someone was sitting in my row. I introduced myself and started connecting with a dude named David. I asked him about his connection with the team and he explained that he was an associate with the title company. He'd worked in the title industry for over 10 years and enjoys it.

Then he asked me the same question, "What do you do, man?"

"I'm working in Operations Support. I'll be handling the systems for the team, make calls to potential clients, and handle lead generation."

"Ah. So you're an important man." David said this in an enthusiastic yet assertive way.

"I guess so. What do you mean?" I asked.

David explained, "You are the one that sets the tone for the transactions. You are very important and that's a huge role you're in. I just met you, but I can tell you are going to do well with it. You have the personality and everything."

"I appreciate that. Thanks."

At first, I didn't believe in how much of an impact my role would make on the team. To me, I was just doing a simple job and making cold calls to real estate window shoppers and creating systems and models for the team. Then, I realized the depth of what David was referring to. Leads would buy or sell homes and converting that lead into a client would mean production for the agent, which would mean production for the team. More importantly, it would mean a transformation of someone's life through buying or selling a home. And it all started with me.

As the night went on, I networked with other people in the suite and watched the basketball players work their magic on the court. Even though it was a home game, I was low-key rooting for the Clippers, and I was in awe of watching Kawhi play and dominate the game. The Wizards were behind at halftime then caught up in the fourth quarter until they weren't able to hold the win. I didn't have a favorite in basketball and yet I was a fan of my new home in Washington, DC.

After the game, I walked to the exit with the group, talked with the McMasters about what to expect for my first day then headed back home to prepare. As I laid in bed that night, I thought about the journey that led up to that night and I couldn't believe it. I came from bumming out on my twin bed in New Jersey playing NCAA football in my room to hanging out with my new colleagues in a suite at an NBA game.

I didn't understand why it took so long to finally land a full-time position. All I knew was that I had the desire for something, and I went after it with everything I had. God knew how to prepare me for this new career and I'm grateful for everything that guided me to that moment in bed. All I could do was take in the present and charge for the future. There is a promise that is yet to be fulfilled and I had the right people, and faith, to push me toward my destiny.

BECOMING
BOLD

CHAPTER 32

Orientation Day- December 9, 2019

The day had come. It was my first day in Washington DC. I woke up early to get ready and made sure I had enough cushion to get from Bethesda to the office on time. I took the metro down and got there in under an hour. It was 7:00 AM by the time I got to Brookland Metro Station and the office was across the street. It was way too early, and I didn't have a key fob yet, so I walked up the street to the Starbucks Reserves and sat down at a table.

Fifteen minutes to nine, I decided to head to the office and wait by the door. It was a brisk December morning, so I prayed that someone would already be there. Fortunately, there was someone walking up to the door as I approached the building and I caught them on time. I told them it was my first day and they had me sit in the lobby. A few minutes after nine, Katie, the Front Desk Manager, came in and told me she'd set me up with paperwork before I headed to my desk. I signed off on some forms, received my key fob, and I was ready to go.

At 10:00 AM, I met with Ashley in the conference room to go over the schedule for the day and it was loaded:

- Sales Team meeting at 11:00 AM
- Lunch and Learn with a title company at 12:00 PM
- Group interview at 2:00 PM
- Get fully operational at the desk for the rest of the day

The sales team meeting was cool. I got to meet the team in full and get a sense of what was expected of us throughout the week. Lunch and Learn was exciting too. I learned about a recent change on the sales contracts that the attorneys wanted to share with the agents. They provided lunch from Potbelly and the sandwiches were good. I still didn't understand the hype behind it and yet I digress. The highlight of the day was the group interview for a potential staff member to join the team. To me, it was odd that I was involved in the decision-making process to hire another operations person on my first day. It was a great experience though. It went well, and the McMasters eventually hired our Operations Coordinator, Jessica. She was a clutch team member that we needed. Her hire completed the operations team that the McMasters needed. Right off the bat, the chemistry between myself, Jessica, and

Shulisa was organic and we were ready to make an impact on the team. For the rest of the day, I focused on making sure my computer was set to go to start on some projects. At the end of the day, I laid my list out for the rest of the week and headed home.

CHAPTER 33

Hitting the Phone-
December 10, 2019

It was my second day on the job and I was already creating new processes for the team. I started putting a system together for the agents to submit new listings to the newly enhanced operations team. This would enable us to create the listing profile on the Multiple Listing Service (MLS) and the agents wouldn't have to spend too much time launching the listing online. Around 11:30 PM, Ashley decided to get me started on making cold calls from the team database. It had been a while since I'd done cold calls and I was nervous and yet her leadership and enthusiasm kept me at ease. We created a simple script for buyer leads and made sure my dialer was active to run numbers efficiently as I went through the call list. From noon to 2:00 PM, I made calls from the list provided to me and did what I could to set an appointment.

The first few calls were my warm up calls, so I wasn't expecting to set an appointment right away. As a matter of fact, I wasn't expecting to set an appointment at all and part of me just wanted to get through the next two hours. Even though I had experience doing door-to-door sales and cold calling, I didn't have enough energy to push me through and I was just going through the motions. I realized I had to change that mindset though and get energized. I got up from my desk and jumped around to wake myself up. I remembered that **motion creates emotion** and if I was going to be the first impression of the team, potential clients had to feel my energy through my voice.

Some leads picked up and said they weren't interested while others just hung up during my intro line. **Some will, some won't, so what? NEXT!** I had to lean on my training for lead generation and remembered that **every "no" led to a "yes".**

One hour into my session and no appointments yet. I took a quick two-minute break and then got back at it. I called the first number and the lead picked up. Her name was Veronica.

"Hi. My name is Asher from Keller Williams. Is this Veronica?"

"Hi. Yes this is. How are you?"

"I'm doing well. Thanks for asking. No one ever does."
Veronica laughed.

I continued, "I saw that you came across our website looking at properties recently. I just wanted to know if you were interested in buying or selling a home."

"Yes I am. It's my first time buying a home and I was looking to see what was out there on the market."

Then I asked what her search criteria was, and she shared her vision for her new home with excitement. We even talked about her job and how life was going for her and we shared a few laughs, too. Finally, we set an appointment for one of the agents to connect with her on the next steps and she was squared away. BOOM! I set my first appointment as an ISA and it was only my second day on the job! It felt so good.

Ashley and Robert cheered for me. I still had 50 minutes left for my call time and I suddenly had this itch and excitement to call more leads. I hit the dialer again and went at it. After a few more no's, I got into a conversation with another buyer who was a Commissioner and a business owner in DC. She was very straight forward with what she needed and was eager to move forward with finding a home. After a few more minutes of rapport building, I set an appointment and got her squared away with a meeting with Robert. AYE! Another one booked for the team! Two in one day and I had no expectation whatsoever! That was the highlight of the day.

For the rest of the week, I looked forward to making those calls starting at noon on the dot and not going past 2:00 PM. I set six appointments in total by Friday and I couldn't be prouder. Making calls was officially my favorite part of the job and I made it a standard to set one appointment a day with a goal of setting three. I had the script, the leads, the faith in myself and God, and the attitude to power through the call sessions. My first week in real estate was a success.

CHAPTER 34

A Holly, Trolley Christmas-December 15, 2019

I was driving down to the office from New Jersey after a surprise weekend visit to see mom at work. Little did I know I was about to have one of the most memorable times at my new job. Every year during the holidays, the Menkiti Group hosted a *Trolley Tour* event for the local neighborhood. The event included fun holiday activities for kids in the office as well as food and drink for all ages. The main attraction, however, was the trolley tour. Prior to the event, families signed up for a timeslot to ride on a trolley and sing Christmas carols at homes with the most Christmas decorations. For each trolley run, the team took turns in leading the tours for the Christmas cheers, along with the trolley drivers. I signed up to do a trolley run around 6:00 PM.

When 6:00 PM rolled around and the guests were all on board, I headed to the trolley and we took off. I explained that we had scheduled stops to visit a few decorated homes and the bus was free to point out other homes they wanted to sing to as well. To get the group ready for the songs, I led a warm-up with scales that sounded like a dying cat the higher I went on pitch. This was done intentionally for comedic reasons. I can actually sing... when I need to.

After my first shift was done, Robert asked if I could do one more tour. I said yes and led the tour with my same routine. The first two tours were so much fun, that I decided to run the shifts for the rest of the night. However, the best shift of the night was the "party trolley". The party trolley was the last tour and started at 9:00 PM where guests could drink alcohol and be more obnoxious. I didn't drink, and yet I had my fun people watching as guests sang the songs and requested that we "stop the bus" for me to knock on doors. I was enjoying the camaraderie. For every house we stopped at during that tour, the homeowners would come out with a platter of shots or cookies to serve to us. The hype from the trolley every time this happened was astounding. There was a moment where the trolly wanted me to knock on a door and the homeowner didn't answer.

When I got back on the bus, one guy started singing, "You're a mean one, Mr. Grinch."

The whole bus burst in laughter.

Eventually, the party bus shenanigans had to end, and we returned to the office for the final drop off. Everyone had a great time, and the Trolley Tour was a success. I helped the trolley driver with one final sweep before heading inside the office for breakdown. We cleaned everything within an hour, and I headed back home to Maryland. Ashley gave me the option to take off work the next day since I served at the event. As much as I appreciated the offer, I decided to continue my grind. The next day, I set four appointments during my call time and finished the week with eight set appointments. No days off for this guy. I have a wedding to make happen.

CHAPTER 35

Running with Giants-
January 14, 2020

Ashley signed me up for a KW training course called *BOLD: Business Objective: Life by Design*. The course is for agents looking to enhance their business through tactics and systems put together by Gary Keller himself and top-producers in the company. Even though I was an ISA, the McMasters thought it would be a good idea to get me into the course and get the most out of it for my call sessions.

The class was held in Columbia, Maryland and I was weary of the drive. Toward the end of December, my car was having gear shifting issues and after a certain amount of time, the engine would downshift and slow the car down. I would have to pull over, turn the car off, and then restart it. I wasn't driving around town much until then. I prayed that I would make it to the session safely. I left an hour and half early, even though it was a 45-minute drive and I'm glad I did. When I was ten minutes away from the meeting center, the car started to decelerate on me when traffic was most heavy on I-95 North. I had to pull over to the shoulder and restart the car. The good thing was I only had a few more minutes to get to the class. The bad thing was the uncertainty of how I was going to get back on the road safely. At the crack of dawn, people were speeding as if their lives depended on it. I waited about five minutes until I had enough time to make a move into the lane and get going. I was worried about the acceleration and yet the car held steady around 55 MPH. Fortunately, the oncoming cars were going slightly slower behind me and merged into the left lane.

I finally made it to the class. I was so relieved once I got on the off-ramp and navigated my way to the training building and parked my car. It was the scariest ride of my life. Thank God for traveling mercies. I waited to go into class until 15 minutes before it began. When I got to the registration table, I was greeted with enthusiasm by a guy named Dylan.

"Good morning man. How are you? Are fully BOLD?" He meant if I was registered for the full, seven week course.

"Good morning. Yes I am, sir."

"AWESOME! Here's your material for the course. When you find your seat, tell Hudson that you are fully signed up and he will give you a sticker. Welcome to BOLD."

When I entered the classroom, there was a sea of red seats and I knew immediately where I wanted to sit: front row. I grabbed my seat, placed my class materials under it and went up to Hudson for a sticker.

"Hey, good morning. Are you fully bold?" he asked.

I replied with excitement, "Yes I am!"

"Terrific. Ring this bell and I'll give you your sticker."

I hit the bell, got my sticker, and put it on the lapel of my jacket.

"There's also some Chick-Fil-A and breakfast items on the table over here if you would like to grab something."

"Thanks."

On Tuesdays and Thursdays, I usually fast from midnight to noon as a spiritual practice. However, I wasn't sure if lunch would be served and I would have to hit up the McDonalds across the parking lot from us and I didn't want to deal with a migraine later on, so I decided to get some nuggets and a cinnamon roll (and no, I didn't feel bad about it). Around 9:00 AM, the class started, and I was excited for what was to come.

"Good morning, everyone, and welcome to BOLD. My name is Hudson and I'll be your BOLD Coach for the next few weeks. I am excited to be on this journey with you."

There was a roar of excitement from the crowd and it was incredible. Hudson was a top-producer from Southwest Florida and he's been in the business for over 10 years. For the next eight weeks, he would be our BOLD instructor and teach us the ways of establishing a strong business and living a life by design. Hudson had everyone in the room introduce themselves, share how many times they were BOLD (meaning how many times they had taken the BOLD course) and what team they were from. It was a very diverse crowd to say the least. For some people, it was their first BOLD class, like me, while others were on their fifth, sixth, or tenth BOLD. Some of Hudson's BOLD staff wouldn't even share their number because of how many times they'd taken it.

Then I realized something - I wasn't in an average training class with average agents looking to excel in their business. I was in a room with the best of the best. These agents had sales volume that ranged from $10,000,000 to hundreds of millions. Many of them also took the course as much as 12 times and they shared how their businesses, and personal life, skyrocketed each time. There was even an agent named Matt from Philadelphia who made the drive to attend the class. It was the closest BOLD class he could sign up for in the season. That's dedication. If Matt was willing to make the drive to be here, I was willing to do what it took to make the most out of the course.

Before we started, and ended each class, Hudson had us chat the BOLD affirmation to get us into the mindset of conquering the day:

> *There is no chance, no destiny, no*
> *fate that can circumvent, hinder,*
> *or control the firm resolve of MY*
> *determined soul. WOOOOO!*

CHAPTER **36**

*Paying it Forward-
January 14, 2020*

For the first half of class, Hudson went over house rules and what to expect for the day. We went into material about mindset, which was awesome for me because of the previous training I had through my Wealthy Dad, Tony Robbins, NLP, and my studies in personal development in college. Everything seemed to overlap, and I felt like I was ahead of the game.

Before our lunch break, Hudson opened an opportunity to the class that I had never seen before. In every BOLD class, there was a need to help people who didn't have the financial support to complete the course and graduate. The first day of BOLD was free to anyone, and yet people would have to pay for the remainder of the program by the end of the day. To help alleviate the cost, BOLD instructors offered the class an opportunity to contribute to a BOLD Scholarship Fund to help those who would like to continue with the course. Several people stood up when asked who needed assistance and then Hudson opened the floor for donations.

The first person who donated pledged $800, the full price of the course. He wasn't able to complete the course due to conflicting schedules and yet he understood the value of it since he'd completed it before. He wanted to pay it forward. Others followed suit and gave hundreds of dollars and I wanted to join in. I had to think about it though because I didn't have a lot. Between my bank account and my wallet, I had $70 to my name. It wouldn't make sense to make a donation and yet I wanted to. It wasn't about the "glory" of giving that I yearned for. It just felt natural for me to participate because I understood the feeling of wanting something and not being able to get it. Sometimes, my family and friends invested in me because they love me and believed that I would make something out of their investment. The McMaster's signed me up for this course because they believed that it would help me be better at my job and in my life. Quite frankly, I didn't really know what I signed up for until that moment. This was more than just business - this was about transformation.

I finally raised my hand and asked Hudson to put me down for $10.

"That's awesome of you. Thank you. Anyone else?"

After a few more moments of heart-felt donations, we tallied up the total and raised $3,060 for the fund. The class cheered and there were a few tears in the room.

I was stunned at what had transpired and I started to see what this course was about. Looking back at the description of the course, it starts off with the following:

> *Choose ABUNDANCE for*
> *YOUR life. Embark on a LIFE-*
> *CHANGING transformation*
> *during this seven-week JOURNEY*
> *by creating a Life by Design.*

When people signed up for the course, they had trust in building abundance in their lives. When we raised the money for the BOLD fund, we experienced sharing abundance with others. To me, abundance is not defined by the amount of money in one's bank account. Abundance is a mindset that can be shared with anyone. I was truly grateful to have taken this course and I was eager to see what was next.

CHAPTER **37**

Going All In-
January 14, 2020

One of the last exercises we did in class was about pleasure vs. pain. The idea behind this exercise was to pinpoint three goals or "actions" we would like to accomplish and associate them in the following categories:

- Pain of taking action
- Pleasure of NOT taking action
- Cost of NOT doing action
- Gain of doing action

The three I chose were:

1. Building a referral pipeline/business
2. Set 30 appointments a month for the team
3. Pay for my wedding deposit

Hudson gave the room 10 minutes to fill in our thoughts for each of the categories before he opened the floor for volunteers to share. Due to the nature of this exercise, things were expected to get sensitive and emotional and yet it was a safe place to open up. Two agents each shared one of their business goals to the group and we cheered for them. Then Hudson challenged anyone to share a goal that wasn't all just business, just to put a twist in the overall message of the exercise. I looked at my third goal and thought, *you know what? I'll share.*

I volunteered as tribute and stood up from my seat.

"Hi, everyone. I'm Asher and I'm first time BOLD."

Clap. "YES, YOU ARE!"

"So, one of my three actions is to pay for my wedding venue deposit. I am planning to marry my fiancé this summer."

Then Hudson had me go through each category and it was written as such:

- Pain of taking action
    - Pick up a part-time job for extra income
    - Researching loans that can cover the cost of the wedding
    - Save a majority of my check, after rent

- Pleasure of NOT taking action
  - Free time for TV at home after work
  - Gym time
  - Spend time with Janay after work
  - Wait on normal paycheck
- Cost of NOT doing action
  - End the relationship as a choice because I wouldn't be able to support Janay
  - Damage my credit further
  - Lose my car
  - Lose my housing
  - No groceries
  - Can't forgive myself
  - Settle for anything
- Gain of doing action
  - Set new wedding date officially
  - Instill belief in Janay (Her smile is what keeps me going)
  - Clearer picture of what the wedding day would be like
  - Internalize the reality of wedding
  - One step close to Thailand for the honeymoon

As I was sharing my pleasures and pains of reaching this goal, I caught myself choking up a little. After I was done, the stillness in the room was very present and the message of the exercise was clear.

Then Hudson said, "Thank you for sharing, Asher. I just want to point out the one thing that struck me the most, which was the cost of not taking action. How he said he would end their engagement because he wouldn't be able to support her. Guys, this is real stuff. This is what pushes us to make things happen."

The room clapped as I sat down, and I exhaled a sigh of relief. As personal and nerve racking as that was, I was glad I'd shared it with the group. It helped me come to the reality that this is a goal I set before me and I would do whatever it took to make it happen.

It was the end of the first day of BOLD and it was time to go home. I decided to take the scenic route this time to avoid heavy traffic in the event my car started to act up again. Unfortunately, I had to pull over twice on the way back and yet I made it home safely in under an hour. As I laid in my bed, I took in the day's events and realized the impact that exercise made on me. I'd participated in similar programs in the past and yet this one was very different. I'd never volunteered to share something so personal to me and not be judged for something that may be nearly impossible to most people. Hudson and the class really supported me and believe that I could make this happen. All I had to do was go all in and see what would happen next.

CHAPTER 38

The Attitude of Gratitude-
January 14, 2020

During the first day of BOLD, we were tasked with a 66-day challenge that emphasized the idea that it takes 66 days to establish a habit. We had a choice in picking an area of our life to focus on and form a habit that supported that area over the next two months. For my habit, I decided to feed my spiritual life. I made a promise to myself that I would write down at least one thing I was grateful for every day before I started work. One reason I wanted to do it was because gratitude is the highest form of energy. Anyone that is truly grateful for anything is someone that is operating at a high level in life.

The other reason is that it's the will of God as stated in 1 Thessalonians 5:18 NIV, "Give thanks in all circumstances; for this is God's will for you in Christ Jesus."

I like this version of the scripture because it's clear that we should be grateful in **ALL CIRCUMSTANCES**. I may have only had $60 to my name during this time and my car was not functioning right, yet it didn't mean that I couldn't be grateful for what I do have now and what is coming my way.

I started off with being grateful for traveling mercies that day. Then, the next day, I wrote down new laundry. Who isn't grateful about a fresh batch of clothes? I ended up writing down more than one thing each day throughout the challenge and I wrote on my gratitude list in the morning on the train ride to the office. That was my time to look back at the previous day and share my gratitude with God for what He's done for me. This attitude of gratitude kept the standard of how I would start my day and opened my awareness that no matter what was going on in my life, **there was always something to be grateful for now and later.**

CHAPTER 39

The Friends I Didn't Deserve-
January 23, 2020

For the next two Tuesdays, BOLD was canceled because of Family Reunion, the company-wide convention. It was a week-long event and nearly everyone in Keller Williams was in Texas networking, learning from each other, reflecting on the last year, and looking ahead. Most of the sales team went and the operations team held down the fort for the week. I don't remember much about this day except that I wasn't feeling 100% the second half of the day. There was a dark cloud that hung over me and I was worried about my car. Even with the newfound source of gratitude I found through BOLD, I didn't believe in it as much as I should have.

I was fortunate enough to make it to the first BOLD session in one piece. There was no way I would risk driving my car in its current condition to the second class. Plus, I was running low on commuter money. I didn't have a lot of cash to reload my metro card and I wasn't sure how I could get on the train or bus. I was piggy-backing off other commuters when going through the metro stalls to and from the platforms. To top it off, I was worried about finding a way to pay for the venue deposit for the wedding. Everything just suddenly hit me that day and it was not a pleasant train ride back home.

The one thing I realized about myself early on is that I bottle things up and hold in my feelings for way too long. I needed an outlet to express those feelings, so I can find a way to get past the worry and doubt and become stronger. I would usually vent to Janay and yet I couldn't wait until she got off her shift, which was roughly around midnight. I needed to vent about my worries, and I decided to go to one of my most trusted groups I was involved with: my mastermind group.

The mastermind was started up by my personal fitness trainer, Craig, around summertime. Through him, I also met three other individuals: Brogan, Solomon, and Nicki. Brogan and Nicki are mom-preneuers in the health and wellness field and were coaches in their own right. Solomon is a personal development coach that hosted his own podcast and is one of the wisest guys I know. I wasn't surprised that most of the group had a passion for health and wellness because that's what Craig's passion is in life. On the train ride home, I vented to the group in our GroupMe about my concerns with the wedding and figuring out how to pay for my car repair. It was at that moment I realized

being vulnerable would be valuable. First, the group showed great empathy and encouraged me to keep looking ahead and to remember how far I had come at that point. Second, they reminded me that I was more than capable of overcoming the situation and to find gratitude in what I have now. Lastly, they made a gesture that I would never forget.

Brogan and Nicki volunteered to help pay for my car repair. When I saw those messages, I choked up and started to tear up. Though I felt embarrassed to have vented to the group, they didn't make it feel like that and they were genuinely coming from contribution.

I hadn't met the group in person, except for Craig, and yet there was a strong connection between all of us that means so much to me. I was truly blessed to have the mastermind and I felt like I didn't deserve them. I thanked Nicki and Brogan profusely and once I found out the estimate of the repair the next day, they sent me the money and the car was fixed by Monday afternoon. I was able to pay them back the following week as soon as my paycheck hit my account.

Because of the generosity and love from the mastermind, I was able to get to the next BOLD class without a problem. If it weren't for being vulnerable, I wouldn't have seen the value behind what true friendship was. This group was vital to my journey and I'm so grateful for their love and support over the years.

CHAPTER 40

The Day the World Went Dark- January 26, 2020

The deaths of Kobe Bryant, one of the best NBA players to have ever lived, and his 13-year-old daughter, Giana, shook the world to its core. Both died in a helicopter crash in California along with seven other passengers. Janay and I found out at the end of a church service we were attending when the pastor announced it. After church was over, we called our families to talk about the news and everyone was in shock. It just didn't seem real. There was no way Kobe and his daughter had left the world in that way. Unfortunately, it was true, and no words can describe how one felt about it. The more I read the updates, the worst I felt for the Bryant family.

You didn't have to be a basketball fan to recognize who Kobe was. He was that strong of an influence in the world and there was nothing but greatness that shined from him. Kobe was a fierce competitor, both on and off the court, compassionate and the mastermind behind the "Mamba Mentality". Per a article I found on Kobe, it summed up his accomplishments as such:

Throughout his 20-year NBA career, he earned 18 All-Star selections, five NBA championship titles, two NBA Finals MVP awards, and two Olympic gold medals. Off the court, Bryant was a published author, philanthropist, partner of a venture capital firm, head of his own media studio, and a dedicated father to four girls.

Kobe's death was a reminder that every day is not guaranteed. What we should treasure the most is the love we share with our family, friends and significant other. No amount of cars, money, sneakers, and jewelry can ever compare to the value of a human life and the moments shared between each other. Moreover, we should also strive to be the best we can for ourselves every day, so we can give our best to others around us. That's what the Mamba Mentality is all about. Being obsessed with what you want to accomplish, and the positive influence it has on others. According to Bryant's autobiography, *Mamba Mentality*, he shares:

"If you want to be great in a particular area, you have to obsess over it. A lot of people say they want to be great, but they're not willing to make the sacrifices necessary to achieve greatness. They have other concerns, whether important or not, and they spread themselves out."

We are all capable of changing the trajectory of our lives with goals that lead us to change for the better. However, if we don't obsess over our goal while obsessing over the reasons why we set such goals, we will always be stuck in our old ways and never breakthrough. Kobe left a legacy that cannot be erased, and my heart still mourns for his family. Let us remember the Bryant family and may we carry Kobe's legacy through service to others and the Mamba Mentality.

CHAPTER 41

The Love of Money, The Lack of Mindset- All of February, 2020

To get the most out of BOLD, the class had accountability groups to stay on top of our goals for the next month. Robert's theory on accountability held true; **you will be accountable to strangers at some point.** For a group to be aligned for success, one of the exercises Hudson had us do was to circle our BOLD values. These values were a list of things anyone could have and yet we had to circle ten values that were the most unique to ourselves. Here's what I picked:

- Commitment: Being obligated or emotionally impelled to a course of action
- Empowerment: Willing to give and accept responsibility and the power to act
- Faith: Firm belief and trust in something for which there is no proof
- Growth: Investment in lifelong learning and personal development

- Honesty: Being fair and straightforward
- Integrity: Words and deeds match
- Legacy: Making a difference today with tomorrow in mind
- Loyalty: Unswerving in allegiance to an ideal, person, cause, institution of duty
- Passion: Intense feeling of conviction/ excitement/enthusiasm
- Simplicity: Lack of complexity or complication

Then, we had to share our individual lists and pick the top 10 values unique to our team. They were:

- Family
- Integrity
- Commitment
- Honesty
- Trust
- Money/Wealth
- Growth
- Passion
- Team
- Change

We called our team the BOLD Commandos, a mix of Team Leaders, operations staff (just me) and lenders. Compared to the rest of the class, our goals were tracked much differently, and we had to get creative in making sure we were accountable. Fortunately, for me, the ISA piece of my job aligned with most of the class material, so it wasn't all bad.

The focus in business for the week was to set ten appointments, which was no problem. The focus in my personal life, however, was finding a way to pay for the wedding deposit, or all of the wedding. Now, I really wanted to go big and find a way to get a lump-sum of the budget covered for the wedding. I knew it was going to be a challenge and yet it was possible. The question was: how far was I willing to go?

I started researching wedding loans from public and private lenders and making sure that the interest rate wasn't too high. That wouldn't matter much though because my credit was shot at that point. When I was unemployed, my credit took a hit on missed or late payments on my credit cards and student loans. It was obvious that my credit management wasn't strong. I still had to keep looking, though. I searched for loan groups on Facebook and joined a group where people were asking for loans of all sizes. I responded to one post of a guy who claimed that he had a substantial amount of investment money he was willing to give and to private message him for more details. In an act of desperation, I messaged him, and a plan was taking place. It just wasn't my plan.

Throughout the whole month of February, I was on a spiral of financial struggle. I was so set on making this wedding happen, that anything with a connection to paying for it caught my attention. The guy that I connected with on the Facebook group was a scammer.

I had a hunch that something wasn't right and yet I still played his game. It wasn't until he asked me for my Social Security Number to "process" my application, where I caught on. I knew I had to stop this nonsense and focus on what I had in front of me for BOLD and work. Of course, I kept on feeding into the desperation for money and foolishly thought that there had to be private lenders that weren't scammers. *There had to be a few, right?*

I connected with another person online, that seemed to streamline the process and promised to deliver the money via Western Union. To confirm the order, he needed $200 so he could "finalize the code I would use to get the money." Even as I write this, I'm just so ashamed of how far I went to get this money. I was eventually scammed $600 from this "lender" and I felt the desperation hit my heart deeply. I knew what I had done at the time and I had to fix it one way or another. Luckily, I screenshotted the transactions made on Cash App and called my bank and explained what happened. I filed a dispute and they credited $600 back to my account until the investigation was over.

For a while, I had a belief that the *love* of money isn't the root of all evil and that it was the *lack* of money that was the root of all evil. During this pathetic mess, I realized that **money IS the root of all evil because of the lack of mindset around it.**

The first half of 1 Timothy 6:10 KJV reads, **"For the love of money is the root of all evil."**

The second half, which I neglected because it wasn't talked about as much and I didn't take the time to dive deeper into the scripture reads, **"Which while some coveted after, they have erred from the faith, and pierced themselves through with."**

I had strayed away from my faith in God when he was providing me the opportunities to come up with the money. It was clear that I had to let go of what I was doing and to let God do what He knows He can do. The love of money spurred all this evil into my life because I lacked the mindset and faith that God was going to provide. He already gave me the tools and vehicle to make it happen and I was stupid to lose sight of that.

The BOLD class was my answer. Working in DC was my answer. Staying in my faith was my answer, and I remembered that moving forward. I would not let anyone, or anything rip me apart from my foundation of faith ever again. I kept my BOLD values, and my faith in God close to me and I would do better moving forward.

CHAPTER 42

Breaking the Phone- February 10, 2020

Before diving into the days content, Hudson would highlight anyone who had done a BOLD 100. This lofty activity is when an agent has 100 conversations in the course of 24 hours and usually wields interesting results. The example that Hudson shared when speaking about the power of the BOLD 100 is when an agent was in the hospital with his pregnant wife and after the birth of their child, he did a BOLD 100 in the hospital lobby while the wife recovered. At the end of the 100 dials, the agent captured over 16 referrals for new business and a handful of appointments with existing clients. At first, I wasn't for it and I had a limited belief that I didn't have the time to do that within my day-to-day. Then, during that class, Hudson handed out pins to the agents who completed a BOLD 100, and had them explain their experience with the campaign and their outcomes. I wasn't sure on how I would succeed in completing a BOLD 100 and yet I knew I wanted a pin.

So, I decided to do one the following Monday before next class. I asked Ashley if I could execute a BOLD 100 and we worked out a plan for me to do calls all day Monday starting at noon. I had my call list set, my Celsius Energy drink, and my vision to get 100 yes's and no's in a course of a day. LET'S DO IT!

Monday rolls around. I come into the office and handle operations support inquiries first. Then we had our sales meeting at 11:00 AM, and at 12:00 PM on the dot, I was dialing away for my 100 contacts. Five dials in and I set my first appointment. Next call after that, another appointment. And another one. And another one. And another one. I was laser focused on getting to 100 conversations. All I needed to hear on each call was a yes or no. The no's were the best part because I was always one away from a yes and I saved a few seconds in between calls. By 4:00 PM, I started to get exhausted. Speaking with clients over the phone takes a certain amount of charisma and is physically and mentally draining after a while. I didn't even eat that day. All I had was my Celsius drink and kept hitting the phone. By the time I got to 70 conversations, I maxed out my database and it was 7:00 PM. I needed 30 more to complete the campaign and yet I had to start heading home before I got locked in the office. I gathered my things and as I headed toward the Metro back home, I started to text and call my personal sphere of influence and asked if they knew of anyone looking to buy or sell real estate. I also messaged people on social media. For the most part, I received referrals from those contacts and by 8:30PM, I hit my 100 contacts for the day.

I texted Ashley and she gave me a shoutout in the team GroupMe. The mission was complete. The crazy part while doing the campaign was that I didn't have to change a thing from my usual call routine. I used the same script, asked the same questions, with minor adjustments thanks to the class, and kept things as simple as possible. The only difference was that I made a commitment that was daunting yet achievable because I put my mind to it. I said I was going to do it and I did.

CHAPTER 43

The Pin and the Win- February 11, 2020

I was halfway through the program and I was eager to learn new material. I was also excited to share my BOLD 100 result to Coach Hudson when class started. Although a piece of me was excited to share my results with the class, I wasn't looking for the glory. I just wanted the pin. When Hudson opened the floor for this week's BOLD 100 testimonies, I stood up and was ready to share my experience. I told the class that it was daunting at first, and it took me eight and half hours to complete.

As he tossed a pin my way from the other side of the room, Hudson asked, "What was the outcome of your calls?"

"I set 15 appointments and received 12 referrals, sir."

The room fell silent, with a few gasps lingering.

In a sarcastic tone to the class, Hudsdon replied, "Oh, ok. So, 15 appointments. 12 referrals. Not a big deal, right everyone? It's not like the BOLD 100 doesn't work, right? Congratulations, Asher. Great job."

I thanked Hudson and took my seat. My team congratulated me as well. As Hudson was getting into the class material, I admired the BOLD 100 pin for a moment, took a picture and sent it to the team GroupMe. I messaged them:

"The power behind this pin is from the power of commitment and inspiration of this team! This is a team accomplishment!"

Although I was the one that made the calls and set the appointments, I wanted to give credit to the team because they gave me a chance and the opportunity to contribute. Thanks to Ashley and Robert for believing in me, I was able to execute goals that pushed me beyond my comfort zone. The BOLD 100 changed the trajectory of how I conducted business moving forward and it would not have been possible without the faith instilled in me.

It took me two days to send out the appointment invites to the new clients. Due to having class all day and the commute in between, that was the most stressful part of the BOLD 100 experience. I even joked with Ashley that I needed an intern to email the appointment invites for me next time. And yes. There was a next time. BOLD 100 wasn't just a lead generation activity, it was a mindset.

CHAPTER 44

Breaking BOLD Goals-
March 6, 2020

The BOLD course was coming to an end and I wanted to graduate from the program with momentum. For the remainder of BOLD, I executed three more BOLD 100s, each yielding between seven to twelve appointments, with a mix of buyer and seller clients. I made the calls every Monday to start the week off strong and left the office around 7:00 PM each time. This was one of the ways to make the wedding happen. The more appointments I set, the more money I would make. At that point, it seemed like the only way to get to the wedding was through BOLD 100s. Some people didn't understand why I decided to do a BOLD 100 three weeks in a row. I wasn't doing it for the pins after the second time. I craved the momentum the campaign came with. The anticipation of the next call and wondering how I could transform a client's life. The discipline instilled within me changed the way I looked at cold calls forever. Additionally, I had something I was willing to fight for and that was to marry my fiancé.

I knew that what I did now in private, I would be rewarded in public.

The symbol of success for me was standing at the altar with Janay and exchanging vows to each other at our wedding.

After a month of hard work and breaking barriers in my workflow, I decided to take a half day from work to drive to the wedding venue Janay and I found in Baltimore. Janay already did a walkthrough a month ago, and it was my turn. I met with the venue coordinator and she gave me a tour of the ceremony and reception spaces. It was everything that Janay and I were looking for and with having the wedding on a Monday, the price was right. The coordinator and I sat at a table in the reception space to fill out the paperwork and lock in the wedding date. Then, I pulled out my checkbook and wrote out a check for $2,000, which was 50 percent of the venue fee. That's right. I just put a deposit down for our wedding. **I had more money at the end of BOLD than when I started, and I completed my goal in securing the venue.** If there was any indication that this was my winning season, it was the moment I paid for the venue deposit out of my own pocket.

When someone has a "why", they can endure any "how". The BOLD 100s set the standard of how I could contribute to business while achieving the goals in my personal life. I would do anything, within reason, to make things happen, especially for Janay. All I had to do was look at what's possible and pray for the strength, knowledge, and resources needed to make it to the top. I wasn't traveling on this path to success alone, and I wouldn't be able to do what I do without the guidance of the leadership at work, the wisdom of the BOLD class, the love from my family, and the grace of God.

CHAPTER 45

Onward- March 10, 2020

This was it. The last day of BOLD. After that, Tuesdays would go back to "normal", although any day in real estate is far beyond normal. I couldn't believe how fast the last few weeks went by and yet here we are. The last day was supposed to be light on material and yet brought some heavy emotions as the class reflected on the accomplishments made throughout. The one activity we did was what I called "Strengths Finder." It was a two-part exercise that asked us what strengths we see within ourselves and to write down as much as we could.

My list was simple:

- Determined
- Faithful
- Fun
- Loving
- Forgiving

- Persistent
- Visionary
- Goal-oriented,
- Service-oriented
- Grateful
- Giving

After a few minutes, Hudson had everyone rip the list out of our BOLD workbook, flip it over and have everyone tape the blank side to each other's backs. The blank side was titled, "Strengths Others See". For the next ten minutes or so, we walked around the room to write the strengths we saw in others on each other's back. With music playing in the background, the exercise was filled with fun, laughter, and pure joy. Everyone had something amazing to say to everyone.

After 15 minutes, Hudson had us go back to our seats to look at our lists in silence before talking about the impact of the exercise. I looked at my list and felt very touched by what was written about me:

- Great spirit and hardworking
- Appointments galore!
- Ambitious and driven
- Brave heart
- Inspiring go-getter
- Sharp dresser and motivator
- Loving
- Shining star in real estate

- Pushing through boundaries
- Role model
- Determined and a calculated risk taker
- Definitely a risk taker
- Hard working with a you-can-do-anything attitude

One person even said, "You are powerful. Your drive is infectious."

I couldn't believe it. The fact that my classmates said these things to me confirmed that everything I had gone through at that point was worth it. The rest of the room was just as grateful. Tears and smiles were shared as everyone looked at their lists. The sense of accomplishment and worthiness filled that room. Everyone was a winner that day.

For the last hour of the class, Hudson and his team set the room to receive our BOLD trophies. He had the captains of each team go up to the middle of the room and pass out the trophies to their respective teammates. My captain wasn't present for graduation, so I had to take the lead as co-captain and present the rewards for my team. I was first to present and proudly announced each team member's name. After everyone received their trophies, Hudson concluded the class with this:

> "Congratulations everyone. I am so proud of you and honored to be your BOLD coach on this journey.

Now, onward you go. Be bold and
keep changing the world."

To close out the ceremony, we cheered our BOLD
affirmation as a group for the last time.

**"There is no chance, no destiny, no fate that
can circumvent, hinder, or control the firm
resolve of MY determined soul. WOOOOO!"**

The class cheered and hugs and high fives were made
across the room. We did it. We all graduated BOLD
and were ready to take on the world with newfound
skills and mindsets. I thanked Hudson for everything
he'd done for the class. His sacrifice of traveling from
Florida to Maryland every week for us was much
appreciated. He told us that we could still reach out to
him for anything after the class was over and we still
talk to each other to this day.

The class wanted to take a group picture before
heading to a local bar for a celebratory happy hour.
After shaking a few hands with some classmates, I
decided to drive back home and relax and reflect on
one of the biggest accomplishments of my life. Onward
we go!

CHAPTER 46

*Life on Lockdown-
March 11, 2020*

Amid conquering my own journey of becoming BOLD, a greater fight was being fought around the world. The Coronavirus, AKA, COVID-19, was spreading around Asia, then Europe, and eventually made its way into America. The virus infected millions of people throughout the world and the World Health Organization (WHO) declared COVID-19 a pandemic. Towns and cities were forced to shut down businesses of all types from restaurants and cafes to museums and hotels. Employees were asked to work from home if possible or were laid off completely until the virus was contained. The Center for Disease Control and Prevention (CDC) was setting guidelines to minimize the spread through "social distancing" and encouraged wearing masks and gloves when traveling. Prior to lockdown, I remember seeing a man in a suit wearing a medical mask and gloves on a train ride to work. I thought he was doing too much at the time. Now, I'm doing the same thing everywhere I go.

Even though there were many signs of how real this disease was, I didn't take it seriously until the Smithsonian Museums were set to close temporarily. Prior to that happening, I felt the initial response to the virus was excessive and didn't make sense. Grocery stores were packed with people stocking up everything they could and the one thing that everyone was bulking up on was toilet tissue. Yes. There was a shortage of toilet tissue in most stores, and I still don't understand why.

For work, people started working from home and came into the office if they had to. I decided to commute to work until March 24. I loved going to the office and it was my place to get the most productivity done. I also had issues setting up my remote access before I could even consider working from home. It took some time to get adjusted with work-from-home life and yet this was something that I had dreamed about when I was first introduced to entrepreneurship. Even though I wasn't running my own business as a full-time agent, I had the mindset of running a business within a business. I was in the client engagement and lead generation business for my team. Just like most real estate businesses in the region, our team had to pivot how we operated to survive the shift in the market. Our operations team worked with our leadership to ensure we can run the business and serve our clients as efficiently and effectively as if the virus didn't happen.

If there's one thing I learned early on in the pandemic is this: **it's one thing to acknowledge fear. It's another thing to honor it.**

While many people were concerned about high-touch points in buildings and worried about recycled air in the office space, amongst other valid reasons, I didn't let the fear of the virus stop me from going after my goals and getting in the way of work. **Most importantly, I didn't let this fear disrupt my faith.**

The year 2020 already started off rough and odd. It felt like we were living in the Twilight Zone. First, the death of Kobe Bryant and his daughter, Gianna. Then, the NBA canceled mid-season due to COVID-19. Then, President Trump was impeached in early January and then acquitted in February. The Democratic debates were under way for the upcoming election. Meghan and Harry left their responsibilities from the Royal Family. Yeah. A lot was going on. However, this lockdown brought many of us a luxury we needed for a while. That luxury was time. This was the best opportunity to hunker down and leverage the extra time to learn new skills, read books, and find ways to optimize our lives from the comfort of our homes. We even had time to slow down and take in what life was like during this unique time in history.

Our team decided to implement the Miracle Morning as a group for 66 days. This was a game-changer for many of us. Starting our days at 4:30 AM or 5:00 AM brought our production to a whole new level. I finished some books I meant to read years ago, and I even received certifications through online courses from Penn State. I would like to share that I am certified in "Best Milking Practices" as well as "Retail Farmers Market School."

These are a few skills that I will later utilize when I get into agriculture investing. I was also studying to earn my Maryland and DC real estate licenses to be more valuable to my team. The licenses would grant me the opportunity to do more for the team such as open house events, listing walkthroughs, and preparing paperwork for home sales. I even shifted my focus on setting more listing appointments for the team and had seven listings come to the market during the pandemic. For the most part, I was living my best life in quarantine and I'm grateful that my loved ones were safe, and I was able to continue work from home. Not even a virus could stop me from conquering my goals.

CHAPTER 47

Shifting Dreams Once Again- April 7, 2020

It had been three weeks since being locked down in my room and things were going pretty well. I'd revamped my Miracle Mornings, thanks to the enthusiasm from my team and started waking up at 4:30AM to start my day. Starting off the day with prayer, gratitude, exercise, and more put me in the position to really conquer my day.

I just finished a Zoom call with my team and was cleaning my room. I heard a vibration on my desk from a text and I saw that I had a missed call from a Maryland number. The voicemail transcript pulled up as well and I saw the words "Evergreen" on it. Evergreen Museum was the venue Janay and I were using for our big wedding day in June. I called the number to see what was up.

"Thanks for calling the Evergreen. This is Laura."

ASHER CARR

"Hi, Laura. This is Asher returning your call. How are you?"

"I'm well. Just working on these requests today and it's getting crazy."

Laura was the head coordinator at Evergreen, which was owned by John Hopkins University. Obviously, we've spoken before when we initially booked the wedding date and from the tone of her voice, I already knew why she called.

"So, I wanted to get back to you and let you know that John Hopkins decided to cancel all events through June 30th. I know it's not what you wanted to hear and I'm sorry."

Although it was heartbreaking, I was prepared to receive this call. I wasn't blind to the fact that there is a pandemic going on in the world and there has been an extraordinary amount of safety measures put in place to help stop the spread. When the virus started to take traction in early March, I called Evergreen to ask what precautions they were taking for upcoming events. At

first, they canceled events through May 31st. The last time I spoke with Lauren, we decided to stay the course and keep the wedding date the same. However, at that moment, I knew I had to be ready for a shift. It was clear that a shift was happening in our economy, and that usually translates to shifts in our personal lives.

I replied, "Thanks for letting me know. I was anticipating this call, if anything, and it's quite alright."

Lauren then gave us options to move the event to another date within 18 months or cancel the event completely and receive our deposit back. I told her I'd talk to Janay about it and we would get back to her. Janay really loved the venue as much as I did, and there was no real reason to pull the money out at that point. I called Janay and told her the news and I knew that she was going to be just as upset as me. It felt like the extra work I put in to secure the venue last month just went down the drain. That was my biggest accomplishment of 2020 so far, and once again, our dream of making this wedding happen shifts.

Like I said before, I was prepared. The pandemic was an external factor we couldn't control. What helped me get through this for Janay and I was perspective and faith. We both worked very hard finding the right venue, caterer, and other components to make our wedding as special as possible and yet the wedding is really for the people we invited. **It's the ceremony that we wanted to have. The ceremony is what makes a wedding special.** It's not about the fancy cocktail menu with the fancy butlers serving the fanciest foods you've never heard of at a fancy place. It's about the sacred commitment between two people who love each other and will walk through the rest of their lives as one with God.

Marriage isn't a matter of claiming the titles of "husband" and "wife", it's a matter of shifting to the mentality of becoming husband and wife. By the time I decided to propose to Janay, it took a mindset shift to see her as my wife and how I could best serve her as a husband. I didn't want to treat her as my girlfriend anymore. I had a desire to grow with her and give her everything she dreamed of and more.

Although we were upset at changing the event date again, we were still optimistic in getting married on paper. Our faith in becoming one, officially, never left despite the circumstances and I knew that through any situation in the external world and our personal worlds, we would get through it together stronger, wiser and full of more love than ever before. Coronavirus, Papyrus, Miley Cyrus. I don't care. I'm marrying my best friend!

CHAPTER 48

Pivot or Panic- May 5, 2020

Nearly eight weeks into lockdown and I was just living my best life. One of the best things to come out during quarantine was the ample amount of time to dive into personal development and education in all areas of life. For KW associates, it was an extra holiday we didn't know we needed. A month into quarantine, KW announced an online training course called *BOLD: Pivot,* which was based on how agents could survive and thrive during the pandemic. It would be everything I learned in BOLD in the beginning of the year plus more and everyone was excited for it. By the time the first online session launched, nearly 40,000 people signed up.

Without hesitation, I signed up a few days before launch and knew that my production level would go through the roof. This also forced me to throw myself outside my comfort zone and stretch my goals. For my ISA activities, I pledged to set five appointments a day for the team, including at least one listing appointment a week. That meant my 30-day goal was to set 106 appointments, with the hopes of 53 being held by the agents. Despite how terrified I felt, I knew that I needed this push, and I was going to do whatever it took to reach my goals. Prior to *BOLD: Pivot*, I realized that I would sell myself short in setting my goals, knowing that my standard was easily attainable.

This reminded me of something my middle school principal shared with my class about success, **"When you reach a certain level of success, you become comfortable and that is the worst thing you can do to yourself. Get comfortable being uncomfortable."**

Once I got a handle on setting appointments at a high level, I started to get comfortable in my production. Even with the BOLD 100s I ran during my first BOLD experience, there was another ceiling for me to break that the quarantine placed. **I was being entrepreneurial again and I had to become purposeful.** It was time to get serious and take a reality check; it was time to pivot.

Over the next two months, I set 100 appointments with 38 clients doing business with the team. Even though I didn't hit my goal, I learned what I had to do in order to accomplish such a task and execute it better in the future. This goal also pushed me to be more creative and test new waters in business and in life. During

BOLD: Pivot, I did a soft launch for my real estate referral business, TouchStone Agent. It was inspired by my ISA work for the team and established an extra stream of income, although I would pass business to the team as well. I spent a small budget on marketing to understand the lead generation and directed traffic to the website. Thanks to my great friend and ROTC college roommate, Kanowitz, I had a fantastic looking website that I loved. Kanowitz runs a marketing business called *Resolution Marketing* and he started it earlier in the year. He worked on my website diligently for a few months before launch and it was worth the wait. In early June, I did a major announcement on my social media and it took off from there, benefitting the team and all those I worked with in various real estate markets.

Despite the current circumstances in the market, our team was able to transform many lives during the pandemic and increase production like never before. For the month of April, the team did $22,000,000 in sales volume, making us number one in the region. It really comes to show that anything is possible in any environment. You just have to be willing to make the adjustments. **It is the set of the sail, not the direction of the wind that determines which way we will go. The same wind blows on us all.** There's no excuse for anyone to not take action in a shifting market and not have some level of production in any aspect of his or her life.

In Romans 5:1-5 KJV, it states:

> "Therefore, since we have been justified through faith, we[a] have peace with God through our Lord Jesus Christ, through whom we have gained access by faith into this grace in which we now stand. And we[b] boast in the hope of the glory of God. Not only so, but we[c] also glory in our sufferings, because we know that suffering produces perseverance; perseverance, character; and character, hope. And hope does not put us to shame, because God's love has been poured out into our hearts through the Holy Spirit, who has been given to us."

In times of difficulty, opportunity is in the midst and God will always provide a way to break through the darkness. It takes a certain person to obtain a certain goal. People have to be different to live differently and in times of trials and tribulation, you morph into the person you have to be to get what you desire. **You either panic or pivot in times of difficulty**. Always choose the latter.

CHAPTER 49

Home is Where the Heart Is- June 1, 2020

Nearly three months after the lockdown, Janay and I decided to go home and visit our families for the weekend. During this time, states were slowly reopening, and we had a chance to possibly secure our marriage certificate in New Jersey. The courts were only open from Tuesdays to Thursdays, so we set an appointment with City Hall for the following Tuesday, and gave ourselves an extended weekend. On a Friday evening, I dropped Janay off at her grandmother's house, where her father picked her up from and then I headed home.

Being home during a pandemic can do a lot to a person. Some people were able to find calmness in their life while others were over it because they couldn't do their child's algebra homework, or they craved going to their favorite restaurant just to get out of the house. For me, the pandemic really slowed things down in my life and put things into perspective. For a while,

I was missing out on spending time with my mother. She's been through a lot to be where she is now, and I felt that she didn't always feel appreciated for her sacrifices and hard work. The more I thought about it in Maryland, the more I realized how much time I focused on the future and not truly living in the now.

Due to the virus, my mother wasn't able to return to work in New York and she's been on a little vacation since lockdown. She needed the break. Traveling from New Jersey to New York throughout the week can take a toll on a person. She has been doing that commute for over 20 years. Ever since lockdown, she's been living her best life, watching her Filipino shows, and taking walks around the block as part of her morning routine.

On Monday, I woke up for my miracle morning and got through my morning reports for work in the living room desktop. Around 9:00 AM, my mom said she was going to do her morning walk. I saw this as an opportunity to spend time with her. I ran upstairs, put on workout clothes, and caught up with her down the block. We walked toward the park, which was nearly a mile away from the house.

During the walk, my mother talked about what she'd been up to and what's been going on at home since my last visit. Some good things, some bad. She just talked about everything. On the way back from the park, she even told me stories about things my Healthy Dad did when I was a baby.

I call my biological dad, Healthy Dad, because he was always focused on my health growing up. He always made smoothies and made sure that my brother and I ate as healthy as possible. My Healthy Dad was into meditation and was skilled in massage therapy. After we got back home, I went back into work mode and got prepared for the sales team meeting. During the meeting, Janay notified me that City Hall cancelled our appointment because the clerk for marriage certification was out sick. We had to reschedule for the following Thursday, June 11th.

It felt good being able to spend time with my mom. It was a great reminder that no matter how far you go in life, nothing compares to being home. You can be the most successful, rich, I-got-it-all, person in the world. If you don't take a look back at where you came from, you'll never get to where you want to be. Never forget where you came from and never forget those who helped you along the way, especially your parents.

CHAPTER **50**

Expanding the Impact-June 5, 2020

During an operations huddle on Zoom, I was going over my to-do list for the day when I was given an opportunity that I did not expect. Ashley tasked me to put a launch plan together in creating an Inside Sales Division for the team. When she told me this, I was excited and yet nervous. I'd never ran a sales team before, let alone created one from scratch. As usual with any massive opportunity given to me, I said yes and figured it out later. Ashley even gave me some references to start my blueprint. I started by listening to an interview of a team that had a successful ISA team that set over 130 appointments a week. Though very impressive, I didn't let that number deter me from what our team could accomplish. I spent the hour taking notes of the interview and it was a solid foundation to putting the project together.

For the following week, I worked on the project for at least two hours a day. I googled what to expect out of a sales team, down to the questions we would ask in the interview process. I even referred to a group project from college, where we created a whole process from marketing our made-up company to creating the hiring process. I had so many resources at my disposal and I was excited to present this plan to Robert and Ashley.

The day before I presented the plan, I spoke with Hudson on what I was working on to get insight on expansion from a leadership standpoint. I did everything I could at that point and yet I felt like there was still something missing.

Hudson told me, **"You don't want to reinvent the wheel so much. You have to find models that work and implement them. Success leaves clues."**

In the book, *Millionaire Real Estate Agent*, Gary Keller talks about using system and models as a foundation of success when building a real estate business stating,

"People have lived before you. Slow down and study their journeys before you start your own. Sound models should be your foundation; then on top of that, add creativity as necessary."

This was a great reminder that learning from what others have done is not only easy but wise, too. To get far in life, you must look at what's been done so you can create what is possible. After the call, I really felt confident, knowing that I had created most of the launch plan based on the one interview I listened to the week before.

The next day, I presented the plan to Ashley and Robert and it was a success. They were just as eager to begin the hiring process as much as I was. More ISAs meant more impact, which meant more transformation in real estate. It meant a lot knowing that they had complete trust in me in bringing this vision to life for the team. This was just another moment that confirmed I was where I needed to be at the right place, at the right time, with the right people.

COMMISSIONED: A DAY TO REMEMBER

CHAPTER 51

The Reflection- June 9, 2011

On June 9, 1994, a two-day-old baby boy was diagnosed with a heart complication at Saint Mary's Hospital in Hoboken, New Jersey, and was immediately transferred to Jersey City Medical Center for better care. Unfortunately, they could not properly care for the infant either and so he was transferred to New York-Presbyterian Hospital, where open-heart surgery was performed. After the surgery, doctors performed a series of tests to look for responses to recovery. Fortunately, the baby responded and was released from the hospital to go home with his parents a month later.

Twenty-six years ago, God brought me into this world through my mother, and at the age of two-days old, I faced death head on. My heart was beating against me, turning me blue and suffocating me to death. I was diagnosed with Transposition of the Great Arteries (TGA) and the doctors had to act fast. TGA is when the two main arteries carrying blood away from the heart are reversed. The typical blood flow in the human body is:

Body-Heart-Lungs-Heart-Body

In my case, the blood flow was
going one of two (wrong) ways:
Body-Heart-Body, without
receiving oxygen from the lungs
or
Lungs-Heart-Lungs, without
bringing oxygen to the body.

Whatever the flow was, it nearly killed me. Fast forward to my junior year of high school, I visited New York-Presbyterian with my mom to see if the surgeon that performed my surgery was still working. Unfortunately, he had retired many years prior, so we took a tour around the hospital instead. It was a massive facility and renovations were being done. There was a chapel in the middle of a wing and my mom wanted to pray before we drove back home. I sat at a pew and did the same. When we were done, she told me that the chapel was the same chapel she prayed in while I was in recovery from my surgery. Out of everything being renovated at the hospital, the chapel had the same layout from what she remembered. It was touching to see the place where the fight for my life was held.

For me, this was a message that no matter what changes on the outside, one's faith should always be the same on the inside. It didn't matter if life was going well, or not. All that matters is that as long as one has faith and truly believes that miracles can happen, there is no doubt that breakthrough is coming.

Hebrews 11:1 KJV says, "Now faith is the substance of things hoped for, the evidence of things not seen."

In Matthew 21:21 NIV, Jesus said, "Truly I tell you, if you have faith and do not doubt. You can say to this mountain, 'Go, throw yourself into the sea,' and it will be done."

Despite the mountains I had faced growing up, my parents always cherished my life as well as my brother and loved us unconditionally. It's the same for every beating heart walking on Earth today. We were all born with a purpose and we all left the hospital for a reason. If there is one thing that will keep us on the course of our destiny, it is our faith. God can move mountains and we can blast through valleys. Don't let anyone or anything hinder you from your greatness.

CHAPTER 52

The Invite- June 10, 2020

Once we found out we could get our marriage certificate in New Jersey, Janay and I decided to have a small ceremony at our church and keep it within the family. In preparation for the event, we went to Wal-Mart and gathered supplies for the wedding favors to be given out at the event. We also pre-ordered our wedding cake at a local bakery back home. Before we started packing to head back to New Jersey, we put the wedding favors together and it was a great date night for both of us. While I was packing my clothes, I was thinking about the wedding and what it would look like. I wasn't really involved with setting up the church or anything, so I had no idea. However, I did have an idea of who would be invited and who I would love to see on my side of the family.

The week before, Janay and I wrote down our guest list of 20 people. At that point, New Jersey had extended mass gatherings to 25 people, which was more than enough to accommodate our immediate family members. Unfortunately, my Wealthy Dad couldn't make it due to the travel restrictions surrounding COVID-19. He did give us his blessing and told me to make the best of the situation. One person I was uncertain of was my Healthy Dad. Since my parents divorced when I was two years old, he missed a lot of major milestones from graduations, getting my drivers license, getting job offers, etc. Part of that was due to his circumstances of not having a permanent home. When I was in elementary and middle school, my mother would drop Aaron and I off at Newark Penn Station where he picked us up for the weekend. There were times when he had more than enough money to take my brother and I out to the movies and arcade. Other times, we stayed in a room he was renting out and played video games all weekend.

Since graduating college, I found myself paying for everything when my brother and I visited him in New York City, where he had been living at a homeless shelter over the last few years. This didn't bother me though. I was at a point where I understood the circumstances and was willing to pay for our food, movie tickets, and whatever else we decided to do for the day. Even though he wasn't there for all the big moments in my life, he's still my dad and he brought me into this life. Plus, we were the only family he had.

For the wedding, I wasn't sure about the logistics of him traveling from the homeless shelter in Brooklyn to New Jersey. The pandemic hit New York City hard and transit services were inconsistent while a curfew was set in place. It was still no excuse to not extend an invite to him though. Janay encouraged me to look into it when we made the list and I decided to invite him. I gave him a call and told him about the occasion. He was excited and said he could be at Penn Station by 8:00 AM on wedding day. For him to say that made me feel better about the whole situation. That would be more than enough time to pick him up and hang out with him before the ceremony. I was excited to see my dad that weekend and have him be involved in the wedding. He deserved that.

CHAPTER 53

The Pre-Approval-
June 11, 2020

One day closer to the big day and we had a chance to finally put it on paper. Janay and I had an appointment at City Hall to prepare the marriage certificate and we were excited. The appointment was at 10:30 AM and we both arrived 30 minutes early to find parking and walked to City Hall together. We also had her cousin with us as a witness to sign off on the certificate.

Upon entry, we had to sign in and get a temperature check before going through the metal detectors. Then we made our way to room B9 to meet with the clerk. In my head, I imagined the appointment as if we were about to do an informal courtroom wedding including us, her cousin, and a judge. I even thought we would have to put our hands on a Bible and swear an oath into marriage. In reality, we sat on a bench in the hallway across from the marriage office and the clerk went in and out of the office to process the paperwork and get our signatures. Ten minutes later, we were good to go and that was it.

We were certified to love, contingent on showing up for the actual ceremony on Saturday where we would need two more witness signatures as well as her father's signature as the officiant. In the language of real estate, we were pre-approved for marriage and our settlement date would be our wedding date.

CHAPTER **54**

Previewing the Dream-June 12, 2020

The day before we say, "I do." It still felt like we had a few more days and yet that wasn't true. It was the fact that I had a whole days' worth of business to accomplish before I could finalize everything for the wedding. That wasn't a problem though. I loved what I was doing for work and I knew it would be a piece of cake getting my activities done. As usual, I started off with updating the business sheets, got on the morning huddle call with the team, followed by an operations huddle, then worked on lead generation and calls to potential clients. I then worked with Jessica and Shulisa on a family game night we were hosting for past clients. That was our big priority for the day, and we took that time to catch up with each other. I also told them about the wedding, since I would be out for the next three days. Their excitement was much appreciated and it really made me want to drop everything else for the day and focus solely on the wedding preparations.

However, I wasn't going to be a scrub and do that, so I kept at my work until 4:00 PM.

Now, it was wedding mode. I checked into the hotel I'd reserved for Janay. Then I went to Target to grab some last-minute clothes for my Healthy Dad as well as little things along the way back home. Once home, I joined the Kahoot game with the team. Then I headed over to the church to drop off sparkling juice for the event and met up with Malcolm. I got to see Janay's mom as well.

"Hello, soon to be son-in-law." There was something about that line that felt right.

Before checking into my hotel room with Malcolm, I took a walk around the sanctuary and saw the reception set up. There was a family-style table setting for everyone to eat at after the ceremony and it looked beautiful. Some members of the church helped the whole day, and they did an outstanding job. Janay and I's dream of being married was coming to fruition right before my eyes, and we had the money to pay for *everything* ourselves in cash.

For the rest of the night, I hung out with Malcolm and Aaron at our hotel. We ended up going to Target again for a last-minute Bluetooth speaker for the wedding before getting Wawa for a super late dinner. When we got back to our room, we ate our hoagies, did a toast with sparkling juice, and watched *Avengers: Infinity War*. Yes. I watched the *Avengers* with my brothers my last night of being legally single. I have no regrets. During this week, it was important to me that everyone involved with the wedding was at ease and didn't feel stressed out, especially Janay.

I wanted to make sure she had everything she wanted, and our families wanted the same. Overall, everything leading up to Saturday worked out very well and everyone was in anticipation of the big day. I was very grateful for that and I was very grateful that God revived this vision for us. I was ready to lead my wife into greatness.

CHAPTER **55**

Living the Dream- June 13, 2020

This is it. The day that Janay and I had been envisioning for the longest time. Our wedding day. Though it didn't have the catering, fancy flowers, and other little details we planned on early in the year, we knew it was better than not having anything at all. Before I could really take in the ceremony, I had a few things to handle for the day. I woke up at 7:00 AM to drop off Aaron back home and pick up my father from Penn Station by 8:30. He got there earlier than planned, so I was the one running late. This gave us more time to go back to the hotel so he can get dressed for the day and take father and son pictures. Malcolm was the photographer/videographer for the day, and he had to be at Janay's hotel by 10:00 AM to capture the make-up artist.

After the father and son pictures, Malcolm and I went to my house for the mother and son pictures. I wasn't sure if this was traditional for other weddings and yet I wanted to capture the moments of my parents helping me get dressed for one of the biggest days of my life, especially at the house.

I was inspired by my friend, David, who got married last August, to take these pictures. When he was getting ready for his wedding, his photographer took pictures of his parents helping him suit up. I thought that was a cool idea, so I wanted to do the same thing for my wedding day. By the way, his wedding was incredible and it was another source of inspiration to work hard for my wedding day.

To me, it was important to capture the essence of how my mom took care of me in the house I grew up in. From getting me ready for school to getting me ready for the wedding, I wanted to have a reminder that home is truly where the heart is.

I will always remember where I came from, no matter how successful I become. Being able to find a loving soulmate and leading a marriage is done in part of who raised the person and I am grateful for my mom and dad for giving me the opportunities to become the man I was meant to be.

For the remainder of the morning, I spent the day with my dad. His belt had ripped, so I made another trip to Target for a new one. Then we got an early lunch at Wendy's before heading to the local bakery to pick up the wedding cake. I wasn't sure if it would be big enough to serve everyone and yet it was. The twelve-inch round cake was heavy and was way bigger than expected. After I got the cake, I headed to the church a little after 12 to get settled and made sure everything else was set.

With the ceremony at 1:00 PM, I was focused on making sure the decorations and everything was set. Fortunately, I didn't have to do much at the church as our family members had everything under control and all I had to do was wait. I was texting Ebonee throughout the morning and making sure they had everything prior to leaving for church. The one thing I was excited for was the limo service that had been arranged for the ladies. Even with the virus eliminating some components of a traditional wedding, I wanted to make the day as special as possible for my soon-to-be wife. Earlier in the week, I arranged a Princess Rolls Royce pick up for Janay, Ebonee, and my new mother-in-law, or as she would prefer to call it "mother-in-love". It would be a surprise for Janay, and it was something she envisioned as part of the wedding day.

When it comes to the nature of being around a Rolls-Royce, you don't purchase one. You commission it.

Per the Rolls-Royce experience: *Begin the journey of commissioning a Rolls-Royce by designing your vision.*

Janay and I had a vision to get married and even though some factors changed the way the vision looked, we ultimately made our dream come true. The love that we share for each other could never be bought. It was in God's timing that we would be appointed as husband and wife.

I couldn't wait for the car to pull up at the hotel and hear about her reaction to it. I gave Ebonee a heads up without giving away what the actual limo would be. When she sent me a picture of the Rolls Royce, it was beautiful and much bigger than I had expected.

Ebonee texted, "Well done, brother."

The ride to church would take 20 minutes.

As time drew closer, my family arrived at church and settled in the sanctuary. My god-parents also arrived. I sat in the Pastors office and waited for Janay's arrival. I made sure I had the wedding ring on me and just sat there in anticipation. Mark came into the office to get ready as well, asking me if I was ready.

Jokingly, he said, "You still have time to walk away."

"Nah, I'm good." I replied as we laughed.

He was just getting me at ease. With each passing minute, I was growing more nervous and anxious and yet excited. Eventually, my mother-in-law and Ebonee entered the office to grab something and to say hi. They enjoyed the limo ride as well. Ten minutes later, it was show time. Mark and I walked to the front of the altar to get in place and our organist began playing the opening song for Janay and her father to walk down the aisle.

As I faced the church doors, I decided to close my eyes for a moment to surprise myself at the beauty that is about to walk down the aisle. Then, I slowly opened my eyes in excitement, and there she was. As they walked down, there was a shadow covering her front side until a few steps in. The natural light coming from the stained-glass windows shined on Janay and revealed a gorgeous white dress and a smile to die for. I thought my heart stopped for a moment. I couldn't help myself from tearing up as she made her way to the altar.

At the altar, Mark initiated the giving of the bride asking, "Who gives this woman to this man?"

Her father replies, "I do."

I nervously reached out my hand to help Janay up the altar before Mark began the invocation and ceremony introduction.

Invocation:

"Family, friends, and loved ones, let us pray together. Gracious God our Father, we give you thanks for your gift of enduring love and your presence here with us now as we witness the vows of marriage between

Asher and Janay. Love has been your richest and greatest gift to the world. Today we celebrate that love. We ask you to bless this couple in their union and throughout their life together as husband and wife. Keep and guide them from this day forward. In the name of Jesus Christ. Amen."

Ceremony Introduction:

"We are gathered here today in the sight of God and angels, and the presence of friends and loved ones, to celebrate one of life's greatest moments, to give recognition to the worth and beauty of love, and to add our best wishes and blessings to the words which shall unite Janay Parrott and Asher Carr in holy matrimony.

Marriage is a most honorable estate, created and Instituted by God, signifying unto us the mystical union, which also rests between Christ and the Church; so too may this marriage be adorned by true and abiding love.

Should there be anyone who has cause why this couple should not be united in marriage, they must speak now or forever hold their peace.

Janay and Asher's lives are given to each of us as individuals, and yet we must learn to live together. In the book of Genesis, God tells us 'Therefore a man shall leave his father and his mother and hold fast to his wife, and they shall become one flesh.' Love is given to us by our family and friends. We learn to love by being loved. Learning to love and living together is one of life's greatest challenges and is the shared goal of a married life. But a husband and wife should not confuse the measurement of love by society's standard of success, even if success is found, only love will maintain a marriage. Mankind did not create love; love is created by God. The measure of true love is a love both freely given and freely accepted, just as God's love of us is unconditional and free.

As you travel through life together, I caution you to remember that the true measure of success, the true avenue to joy and peace, is to be found within the love you hold in your hearts. I would ask that you hold the key to your heart very tightly.

While it was the various roads you traveled on during your time at Penn State University that allowed you to cross paths. While movie nights, ministry and road trips provided an opportunity for you to both share and create countless valuable memories. It is love, which brings you here today, the union of two hearts and two spirits. As your lives continue to interweave as one pattern, remember that it was love that brought you here today, it is love that will make this a glorious union, and it is love which will cause this union to endure."

After a solo from Ebonee, Janay's father took over the remainder of the ceremony for the vows, exchanging of rings, and benediction.

The Vows

"Dearly beloved, we are gathered here in the sight of God, and in the presence of family and friends to join together this man and this woman in Holy Matrimony, which was ordained by God himself, when he said, "it is not good that Man should be alone. I will make him a helpmate. Therefore a Man shall leave his father and Mother and cleave to his wife, and they shall be one flesh.

Therefore is not to be entered into unadvisedly or carelessly, but reverently, joyfully and in the love of God. Into this holy estate these two persons present come now to be joined.

If anyone, therefore, can show just cause why Janay Parrott and Asher Carr cannot be lawfully joined together, let them speak NOW or forever hold their peace."

Silence filled the room. As it should. For the vows, we decided to recite the traditional vows and save the personal vows for the following year.

Her father continued, "Forasmuch, then as nothing hath been shown to hinder this Marriage I ask you, Asher Carr to repeat after me."

I, Asher, take you, Janay Parrott, to be my wedded wife. To love and cherish, For better or worse, for richer or poorer, In sickness and in health. Forsaking all others, I pledge to you my faithfulness, unto death due us part!

During the vows, I found myself choking up midway and I had to catch myself to keep pushing through. It was hard not to think about how far we had come and most of our family had no idea what had happened over the last year.

Then, it was Janay's turn to say the vows.

I, Janay, take you, Asher Carr, to be my wedded husband. To love and cherish, For better or worse, for richer or poorer, In sickness and in health. Forsaking all others, I pledge to you my faithfulness, unto death due us part!

Janay choked up during the vows as well. Just having that understanding together really touched us and being able to make this wedding happen was a testimony that hard work and strong faith can lead anyone to their destiny.

The Blessing of the Rings

The Pastor continued, "Bless, O Lord, The Giving of these rings that they who wear them, may live in your peace and your favor all the days of their life, through Jesus Christ our lord."

The Exchanging of the Rings

"Asher and Janay as you place this ring on each other's finger I ask that you repeat these words: This ring is my sacred gift to you. A symbol of my Love. A sign that from this day forward and always, my Love will surround you. With this ring, I thee wed in Jesus name."

"May the Lord Bless these rings which you give to each other as your sign of Love, Devotion and everlasting peace. Amen."

Closing Prayer

"Oh, eternal God Creator and preserver, Giver of all spiritual grace, the Author of everlasting life; Send thy blessing upon these thy servants, this man and this woman, whom we bless in thy Name; that they, living faithfully together, may surely perform and keep the vow and covenant between them as symbolized by these rings as a token and pledge, and may ever remain in perfect love and peace together and live according to thy laws. Amen."

Pronouncement

The Pastor concluded the ceremony with an exciting tone that sent shock waves through us.

"For as much as Asher Carr and Janay Parrott have consented together in holy matrimony and have witnessed the same before God and those present, and have pledged their faithfulness, each to the other, and have declared their love by giving and receiving rings and by joining hands, I now, by the authority committed unto me as a minister of the Gospel and the laws of the state of New Jersey I declare that Asher and Janay are husband and wife according to the ordinance of God, in the name of Lord Jesus Christ. Those whom God has joined together, let no one put asunder. Asher, you may salute your wife."

With cheers in the background, I kissed my new wife and sealed our fate to eternal love.

"Ladies and gentlemen, allow me to present to you, for the very first time, Mr. and Mrs. Asher Carr."

We turned to our family to the sound of joy. **WE DID IT!** Everything we had gone through together led to this very moment. Standing at the altar as husband and wife. This was my symbol of success. We walked down the aisle in triumph and took in the glorious moment of being a married couple. The love that we have for one another kept us on this wild path to the altar and I wouldn't have done it any other way. After everything we've been through, God brought us to this day on His timing and we couldn't be any happier. God commissioned us as husband and wife, and we were ready to continue our love for eternity. We were victorious!

CHAPTER 56

Beyond the Dream-
June 14, 2020

The next morning, I was packing the car as my new wife and I were heading back to the DMV for the rest of our mini-moon vacation. When I closed the trunk to head back inside the hotel, I took a moment and looked at the building we were staying at. It was a 4-star boutique hotel and we stayed in their best suite. Even though it was only for the night, it was an experience I didn't take for granted. The experience of being able to afford a hotel suite of that caliber and sharing that experience with my new wife. A year ago, we weren't even sure how we were going to pay for a wedding and yet God came through.

I remember Donna telling me, "One thing I have learned is that life will throw you curveballs and take you off track, even when you think you are prepared. Life is full of peaks and valleys."

With that being said, I know that God can bring us through those valleys, so we can continue to enjoy life at its peak. If we were able to have a wedding amid a pandemic and made it as grand as possible, I can only imagine what the next wedding will be like. Fortunately, we had most of the bigger wedding planned in Baltimore and we were ready to work toward that goal again. Or maybe we'll buy a house instead. That sounds like a better idea. I wasn't worried though. It was all about taking in the present and appreciating the gift of life has brought to us.

As we took off to Virginia, all I could feel was the gratitude and love that dwelled in my heart for God, family, and business. Anything could happen in a year and what a year it has been. No one knows what is coming next. All I know is that only God can do it and that this is the beginning of a new end.

EPILOGUE

A year ago, I was working in finance and making decent money. Then I was let go a year before I was planning to get married. I didn't know how I was going to do it and yet I knew I wouldn't be unemployed for long. Then, God brought me through this roller coaster of blessings, lessons, challenges, shifts, trials and tribulations and here I am writing about my journey in my room in Maryland, with the hope of inspiring at least one person to be bold enough to go after what he or she desires. When it came to finding success, my Wealthy Dad always reminded me of this golden nugget:

Be careful of the person you become in the pursuit of what you want.

Since college, I knew what I wanted and yet the person I was changing into wasn't what I desired to be. My thought patterns, habits and vision weren't enough to get me where I really needed to be. Chasing money wasn't enough to be the person I needed to be to make the impact I wanted to leave in the world. Money isn't a goal; it's a by-product of what I did through the actions I took. Working in finance made me realize that there was more than just crunching numbers and working for the top firms in the industry. Getting let go from my last job was the birthday gift I didn't know I needed, and knowing that I have a roof over my head in another state a year later is a testimony to the faith that's instilled in me since day one.

Proverbs 16:9 KJV states, "A man's heart deviseth his way: but the LORD directeth his steps."

In my heart, I knew that I wanted to be in real estate. In my heart, I knew I wanted to make a change in people's lives through real estate and yet God directed me to where I needed to be so I could use my gifts for a higher purpose. Sometimes it made sense, and other times it didn't. And yet, when you trust in God, when you cast all your cares unto the Lord, when you believe that you will receive, God will pour abundance into your life. He will provide in ways you can't even fathom. He will let the blessings flow into your life so much that it will overflow.

A year ago, I was facing uncertainty, and living in faith. Now, a year later, I am living in clarity andI am living in faith. It doesn't matter what winds will come your way, as long as you set the sail toward faith. It doesn't matter who believes in you, just believe in yourself and God. I don't know how to explain some of the things to you on this journey and yet I can tell you one thing: this is my testimony.

I was born with a broken heart. God mended it back whole. I was challenged in my mind. God brought me wisdom. The system told me I couldn't do it. God gave me the strength to conquer it.

Let me remind you that no weapon formed against you shall prosper. This is a battle that God has already won. No matter what comes your way, always stay the course because this is your winning season. Your breakthrough is coming. You were born to thrive, and you were born on purpose. My wish for you is to be BOLD and go after your dreams. My wish is for you to stand in faith, not in fear, and believe that you will achieve. My wish is for you to break out of your comfort zone and break into your blessings. You are only one call, one prayer, one day away from the breakthrough you deserve. The best is yet to come, and I know that you will make it.

Be strong. Have Faith. Be BOLD.

My name is Asher Carr and I am BOLD!

First Year In Real Estate Contribution & Production

626 Appointments Set
$10,300,000 in Closed Sales Volume for the Team
$274,000 in Gross Commission Income for the Team
Three time BOLD and BOLD: Pivot Graduate
Four BOLD 100 Pins Earned
One Beautiful, God-given Wife
All Glory to God

BONUS CONTENT

Get a deep dive into the success principles and
habits shared in this memoir by purchasing:
*Coming From Contribution: A Companion
Playbook to From Broke to BOLD*
Read on for a sample chapter from the Playbook

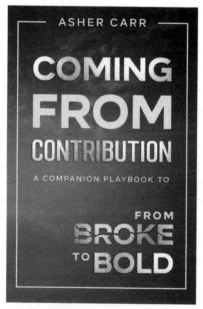

**Available exclusively for download on
Amazon.com and Ashericarr.com**

SPEAK LIFE INTO EXISTENCE

Throughout the story, I mention the use of affirmations, especially when I'm about to enter into a job interview. I started doing affirmations my junior year of college when I was fighting depression and had little confidence in myself. My Wealthy Father told me that I had to start loving myself and appreciate the gift of life God has given me. One way to show that appreciation is through affirmations.

A mentor of mine once said, **"The words that follow 'I AM' follow you."**

It's very true.

A statement starting with "I Am" is a powerful way to elevate your self-esteem or shoot it down. I recommend elevation. Every morning, I started reading a list of "I Am" statements that made me feel good about myself and put me in a positive state of mind. With time, I started to notice a boost in my confidence and I was more aware of what I was speaking into my life. This was a game-changer for me in college and it's just as vital in my life now.

I also implemented Question Seekers into my personal development routine. Question Seekers are questions one can ask themselves and "trick" the mind to seek the answers.

In other words, **where attention goes, energy flows.**

The scripture of Matthew 7:7 KJV says, "Ask, and it shall be given you; seek, and ye shall find; knock, and it shall be opened unto you."

Question Seekers compliment affirmations on the journey to success. While your heart leads you, your mind will follow the clues to the answers you seek. In my experience, asking such questions brings creativity and intention when seeking the answers in anything I did. Below is a set of my old affirmations with a few Question Seekers that you can use. I encourage you to write your affirmations that match your desires. Start speaking victory and confidence into your life everyday for at least a week and experience the gifts that God has set for you.

Affirmations and Question Seekers

*Dear God, thank you for this day and
the gifts that You bring on this day*

*Thank you for waking me up to fulfill my purpose
I am well, I am healthy, I am happy, I am beautiful.*

I am wealthy, I am rich, I am prosperous,
I am content, I am blessed.
Why do I have avalanches of abundance
flowing down on me, so that all my dreams,
desires and goals can come true?
I am love, I am light, I am life, I
am wisdom, I am peace.
How can I be a source of love, joy, peace
and happiness for those around me?
I am highly focused, I am strong, I am
confident, I am courageous, I am creative.
What skill can I learn today to get
me closer to my goals?
I am young, I am youthful, I am radiant, I am attractive.
I am a good listener, I am a great friend,
I attract the best people into my life.
How can I be a great friend to others and be
a catalyst to others success stories today?
I am the best at what I do. I give my
best to life everyday, and I get the
best from life everyday. My days are full
of joy, peace, laughter, and happiness
I attract the right people into my life. I have
many wonderful, caring, and faithful friends.
Love, freedom, money, success, happiness, and
abundance of everything are flowing into my life now.
I am a conqueror
I am BOLD

Asher Carr Collection
Books & Ebooks

Rise From the Ashes Playbook: Setting Yourself Up
For Success In College And In Life Kindle Edition
Coming From Contribution: A Companion
Playbook to 'From Broke to BOLD'

ABOUT THE AUTHOR

Asher Carr is a first-generation college graduate with a passion for serving people through the world of real estate, and inspirational speaking. During his college career, Asher's success as a business major earned him multiple awards and accolades for his character, scholarship, student leadership, and citizenship. After graduating from Penn State Altoona in 2016, he started his career in financial operations before shifting to real estate operations in 2019. In his first year as a Client Engagement & Operations Coordinator, Asher brought in millions of dollars in closed sales volume for his team at Keller Williams Capital Properties, a top 1% Keller Williams brokerage in Washington, DC. Asher is also a licensed Realtor in New Jersey, Maryland, and Washington, DC. Through real estate, Asher learned the art of *service before sales* under Keller Williams and continues to transform the lives of clients by meeting and exceeding their needs. As a speaker, he leverages his faith, and wisdom to spread optimism and passion for inspiring others to create their success stories through faith, family, and business.

CPSIA information can be obtained
at www.ICGtesting.com
Printed in the USA
LVHW012028160621
690399LV00019B/1072

9 780578 916354